the man behind

THE BADGE

a memoir

LEROY GREEN JR.

CLAY BRIDGES
PRESS

The Man behind the Badge
A Memoir

Published by Clay Bridges in Houston, TX
www.ClayBridgesPress.com

ISBN-10: 1-939815-50-9
ISBN-13: 978-1-939815-50-7
eISBN-10: 1-939815-80-0
eISBN-13: 978-1-939815-80-4

To my wife, Lonia, my angel from heaven,
sent by God as my helpmate, till death
do we part.

Live joyfully
with the wife whom you love all the days of
your vain life which He has given you under
the sun, all your days of vanity; for that is your
portion in life, and in the labor which you
perform under the sun.
—Eccles. 9:9

I will love You O Lord, *my strength.*
The Lord *is my rock and my fortress and my deliverer;*
my God, my strength, in whom I will trust;
my shield and the horn of my salvation, my stronghold.
I will call upon the Lord,
who is worthy to be praised;
so shall I be saved from my enemies.
—Ps. 18:1–3

Table of Contents

Introduction

Throughout life, we face many challenges, requiring that we make critical life decisions—from choosing a career to choosing where we live to choosing how we interact with others. Overall, I believe that if we choose to give our lives to God, He will guide us on life's pathway.

Chapter 1: The Beginning

I was born on May 18, 1951, to Florence and LeRoy Green Sr. I was the second oldest of nine children. We lived in a neighborhood in the West Bottoms of Kansas City, Kansas, near the Kaw River. Ours was a small, close-knit community comprised of African Americans, Hispanics, and Cherokee Indians, as well as Croatian, Polish, Russian, and German Americans.

Looking back on my childhood, I realize that many of the men in my community were stand-up people who took responsibility for their actions, whether good or bad. They worked hard to take care of their families no matter the cost, sometimes working two jobs. I want to thank those men for providing leadership and guidance and for showing me how to take responsibility for my actions. By their examples, those men taught me how I should act when I grew older and got a job: work hard, be honest, and tell the truth no matter what the circumstances might be. They taught me to first find a place to live, and then think about getting married and starting a family.

Our community was very family-oriented, and people pretty much got along with each other. Don't get me wrong—people sometimes had disagreements with each other, and we certainly had our likes and dislikes, our ups and downs. But as the expression goes, "when push came to shove," we looked out for each other, our neighborhood, and especially the neighborhood children. Though we may not have used the term, we already had a *neighborhood watch*. Our neighborhood watch consisted of watching over our children, each other, and our property. The adults watched over the neighborhood children as if they were their own children. If children were disobedient, they were spanked and disciplined by parents in the neighbor-hood watch group. I can still feel some of those spankings!

As I walked about in my neighborhood, I would hear casual conversations about all kinds of topics. For example, the neighborhood kids would talk about people and racial topics, mainly in a joking manner, saying which skin color, race, or dad was better than everyone else's. They would say exactly what was on their minds: "I can whip you" or "I'll get my big brother to beat you up." But for the most part, the kids all got along with each other and played games such as softball, football, and hide and seek. My favorite game was when we gathered outside and tried to imitate our favorite cowboys from the shows we watched on television: *Roy Rogers, Gunsmoke, Wyatt Earp, The Lone Ranger, The Texan, Bat Masterson, The Rifleman, Sugarfoot, The Cisco Kid,* and my favorite, *Ringo Kid.* Ringo was the fastest gun of all. When we went outside to play cowboys, we called ourselves the "West Bottom Boys," and we had a saying: "You never mess with those West Bottom Boys."

At Christmastime, most of the boys would ask for a cowboy gun and hol-ster, so we could imitate our favorite cowboys. After receiving our Christmas presents, we would dress down to look as much like our favorite cowboy hero as we could. I mean, we dressed down—from cowboy hats to gloves on our hands to boots on our feet, and we topped it all off with a sassy walk and a swagger in our talk. Our hats were tipped down in front, and we had our toy guns tied to our legs like the real Western gunfighters. Then, we would have gunfights to see who had the fastest draw. Well, I hate to brag, but I always had the fastest draw. After a victory, I would twirl my gun on my finger just like the real cowboys did after a gunfight and then put it back in my holster.

Pretend gunfights were just one of our favorite games; we also imitated other television shows. Tarzan was another favorite hero of mine; no one in the neighborhood could play Tarzan like I could. Of all the boys in the neighborhood, I had the best Tarzan call, including the yodeling sound. In the television show, Tarzan had two different calls. His first was to warn the animals to leave the area because of danger, usually game hunters who killed for sport. His second call was a love call to Jane telling her that he was on his way home and, of course, Jane would answer Tarzan with her own call. Tarzan's love call was the one I did best.

I had many pretend *Tarzan* adventures. I would dress like the safari hunters, and attempt to hunt rabbits, dogs, cats, squirrels, birds, pigeons, and even a frog or two. I made my own bow, arrows, and spears. I acted like a big game hunter, just like the ones I watched on *Tarzan*. Since we lived close to the stockyards, occasionally a bull or cow would get out and run through the Bottoms where we lived. Each time I heard that a runaway animal was headed toward James Street, the main street in the West Bottoms, I would gather my spear, bow and arrows, and a wooden sword, like the big-time game hunter on *Tarzan*. The hunt was on, as I traveled along the riverbanks and through the West Bottoms looking for the runaways. I hid in the tall weeds, just like the natives did on *Tarzan* when they helped the game hunters flush out the animals. Most of the time, I came back empty-handed, but there were a few times when I located the animals. When I located a runaway, I would watch the animal from the bushes until the animal control people came to take the runaway back to the stockyard. When they arrived, I would jump out of the bushes to show them that I had this; I would tell them that I had kept watch over the animals. As they looked at me dressed in my makeshift safari hunter outfit, the Animal Control Officers usually gave me a half-smile and said, "Thank you, son; you did a good job." That always made me feel proud.

I do recall turbulent times in my neighborhood; sometimes, people of all ages fought with each other. After the fighting was over, no matter who won or lost, everyone apologized to each other. All the participants involved in the fighting would gather at a certain location to talk about the fight, just like the sport commentators on television would do after a boxing match. During this time, some agreements were finalized. Afterward, everyone would come to an understanding, apologize to each other, shake hands, pat each other on the back, and give a hug and a friendly smile. Peace would be established all over again, and everyone would walk to the neighborhood store. The kids would buy a pop or an ice cream bar while the adults would go to another place and have a cold beer. Thinking about it now, the way the fights ended was the best thing that could have ever happened.

Shattered Innocence

As a little boy, I also had sad and emotional times; my life growing up in the West Bottoms of Kansas City, Kansas, was not always fun and games. Even now as I write about what happened to me, I become very emotional and tearful. When these sad memories began to surface, I shed some heavy tears for a while; then I prayed, "God help me." You see, I was a victim of a sex predator, not once but twice, by two different men. These incidents occurred first when I was a young boy and later when I was a teenager. Until now, I have kept this part of my life secret. Growing up back then, we were taught to deal with our own problems. My dad and the other men in my neighborhood taught me that no matter what my age, circumstances, or consequences, I was to stand up and behave like a man. Later, I discovered that I was not the only victim of this type of assault in my neighborhood; a few other young boys were assaulted and beaten by the same man who lived in our neighborhood. Those boys did not tell anyone either, but you could see the evidence of the beatings on their faces. Right now, I can only talk about myself and what happened to me.

The first predator took advantage of unsuspecting kids at play. During the day, all the kids would play in their yards or in the fields close to our homes. The fields were covered with tall weeds and sunflowers, and we enjoyed running through the weeds and making paths like a jungle trail. Some of us would have fun climbing trees and jumping out of them onto the nearby dirt piles. But one day, an older man, who I believe was in his early twenties, started coming around every day watching us play games with each other. He started getting involved in our playtime, showing us how to play football and baseball the correct way. He also started taking us down to the neighborhood store and buying us snacks, and he would buy us ice cream when the ice cream truck came through the neighborhood.

One day when I went outside to play, I noticed a small tent set up in the field among the trees and tall sunflowers. As I got closer to investigate, I saw that this same young man was inside the tent lying down. I was not only puzzled but fascinated to see a camping tent in the middle of the field. The young man saw me out playing and asked how I was doing. I answered him in a low, I don't want to speak to you kind of voice. This man continued

6

speaking to me, asking if I would like to come and see what it was like inside a tent. I hesitated for a moment, but he continued on with his conversation, saying, "Don't be afraid, I won't hurt you." This man continued to say, "Look what I have inside the tent, some chips and candy. Come on in and see what it looks like inside." The enticement of the goodies he had inside excited me, enticing me to make up my mind very quickly. I decided to go inside the tent. I let my guard down, went inside the tent, and ate candy and chips while we started talking about kid stuff. We mostly talked about the type of toys and games I liked to play and my favorite cartoon shows on television. For me, the first day was fun and cool. But later, when he thought that I was feeling comfortable, the visits became a little more intense. He started touching, rubbing, grinding, and other sexual acts that are involved in sexual assaults, while I was busy playing with toys and games. Then, instead of chips and candy, he started giving me two to three dollars a visit, saying, "This is our little secret."

Back then, that was a lot of money for a little kid. He gave me money to keep me quiet and to take my focus off what he was doing and what was happening to me. He was grinding on me from the back and front while he was touching my penis in every way. These sexual attacks continued along with an increased amount of money to keep me coming back. That's when the sexual acts performed on me became more intense and frequent, including penetration and oral sex. These acts became so forceful and painful that I cried, yelling for him to stop, to leave me alone. He was hurting me, and I yelled for somebody to help me. Finally, he decided to stop before someone heard me crying and calling for help. He quickly left the area, leaving me in the tent alone, hurting and crying.

I have not told anyone about those abusive encounters until now, 50 years after they occurred. But with the help of God and the Holy Spirit, I can finally tell my story. After being in law enforcement for 31 years, I now know the magnitude of sexual assaults. Processing this part of my life was very painful and emotional, causing me to cry. When I stopped crying, I went into deep prayer and asked God to please help me tell my story. God heard my prayer and immediately sent the Holy Spirit to comfort and guide me as I continued to write this book.

In my adolescence, several incidents had a significant impact on my life. First, I fell victim to a second sexual predator. This time, the predator was an African American male in his early twenties who played ball with the neighborhood boys every day. One day while we were playing ball in the streets, he approached me and asked if I wanted to go with him to the store for some candy and ice cream. I agreed, telling the other kids that I would be back after I went to the store with this older guy. When we arrived at the store, he bought me all the items he had mentioned, and we stayed around the store for a few minutes, until he asked if I would like to go up the street to a tall building. He said we could ride an elevator to the top floor and look down at the city. Once again, I said yes because I had never been on an elevator twenty floors high. I was happy, excited, and having fun. When we exited the elevator on the top floor, I looked out the window at the landscape around the city. I was able to see an outstanding view of downtown Kansas City, Missouri; it was a lot of fun to look down from the top floor at the cars, buses, and people. He asked me to get up on the rail so that I could see more of the city and neighborhood. I was afraid of falling off the rail, but he held me in front of him while I stood on the rail. Then, I realized he was grinding on my butt while he was talking, showing me different buildings and other landscape areas at the same time. The rail was just the right height for him to grind on me.

This abuse occurred several different times until my mom found out what was happening and where he was taking me. I believe some of the other kids told my mom because they knew this man's behavior. She told me not to have anything more to do with him, and I stopped. I want to thank God for sending me a loving, caring mother who saw the writing on the wall and stopped the process at once before it became worse. Let me say this to all those men and women who have been sexually violated during their childhood and teenage years, it's time for you to talk to somebody about your experience—a family member, your close friend, your pastor, or a therapist—to get help for the abuse you suffered. Getting help will make a big difference in your life as you move forward. As I learned, alcohol, drugs, fighting, and having parties all the time are not the answer. Talk to God and you will find the answer.

Another bizarre incident happened to me when I was around 12 years old; this one could have left a bad mark on my life and resulted in a criminal record. Several of my siblings and I were at my grandma's house when she became very angry, fussing and cursing at all of us. She wanted to know who had stolen her money from underneath her clothes cabinet. We told Grandma that we did not steal her money, but she said somebody had taken around $1,500 in cash. When she said she was going to call the police, we got scared, and we went home and told our mom and dad what had happened.

Later that evening, my dad came to me and told me to say I had taken the money. When I told him repeatedly I had not taken it, he said that he knew that. However, he still wanted me to tell my grandma that I had taken the money to keep her from calling the police. My dad advised that since I was a kid, the police could not do anything because I was too young to go to jail. I went along with Daddy's plan and told my grandma that I took her money from underneath the cabinet. She yelled at me and said she was calling the police and that they were going to take me to jail and lock me up. When Grandma said that, it scared me very much. I became sick, shaking and crying, because Grandma kept telling me over and over that I was going to jail. She asked me what I had done with all that money. I did not know what to say because I had not taken it. Nevertheless, I told her what Daddy had told me to say. I said that I had bought candy, chips, soda pop, some toys, and a bicycle.

That's when my great-grandma stepped in. She told my grandma that they both knew that I had not taken the money. I was too small and not strong enough to have lifted the heavy cabinet off the money. Furthermore, she said that they knew it was Grandma's own son—my daddy—who had taken the money. But that did not matter to Grandma because she was angry and very upset. The police were still called, and I was taken into custody by the juvenile authorities and transported downtown for questioning.

When I was questioned by the detectives at the juvenile division, I told them the same story that Daddy told me to tell Grandma. The detectives did not believe my story either. They kept asking me who really took my grandma's money even though I kept telling them that I was the one who had taken it. During the investigation and questioning, Grandma called the detectives and advised them she was not going to press charges against me and asked them to let me go. I was released soon after her call. Later, I realized that my dad had taken the money from my grandma. After that incident, Dad even made me steal money from my grandma's purse several times and give it to him.

Troubling Behavior and Helping Hands

There were a few other examples of troubling behavior when I was boy. I would climb over the junkyard fence, pick up loose iron, throw it over the fence, and hide it in the weeds. Later, I would load the iron in my wagon and take it to the junkyard entrance, where I would sell all of it back to them as found junk. I found other ways to test the boundaries. During the week, when everyone was at work or away, I would walk around the neighborhood looking for unlocked doors. Back then, people seldom locked their doors because they trusted their neighbors, and there was not as much crime as we have today. When I found an unlocked door, I would go inside and snoop around. I did not take anything, but I did eat food, such as cereal, candy, chips, and opened lunch meat in the icebox. After I finished looking around, I would leave, closing the door behind me. On the weekends, I would go to the cement company, located behind our house. If I found a truck unlocked with the keys in the ignition switch, I would start the truck and take it for a drive. I would only go about half a mile before leaving the truck.

When I was a little older, I had a job working in one of our local grocery stores. I found that the boss, Joe, kept extra money in a cigar box behind the front counter. Satan tempted me to take a few dollars out of the cigar box and buy myself some chips and candy. At the time, I didn't know whether the boss knew I was taking his money. But one day, when we went to lunch, I bought the boss's lunch with money that I had stolen from his cigar box under the counter. He seemed surprised and thankful when I bought his lunch. However, days later, Joe called me up to the front of the store and asked me where I had gotten the money to buy his lunch. I told him that I had been saving my money; he did not believe me. In fact, he accused me of taking money from the cigar box. Joe gave me a stern lecture, but he allowed me to keep my job. He told me that he had known I was taking money out of that small box behind the counter. He said that if I had needed money, I should have just asked him. He told me to never take anything from anyone that did not belong to me; he said I needed to work for what I wanted. Joe taught me a valuable lesson for which I am thankful. Over the years, other people, like Joe, helped to make my life a little less difficult when I was growing up.

Although I did not participate in gang activity, living part-time in the projects exposed me to gang violence and crime. The violence usually started on the weekends. Sometimes, the gangs would face off against each other in the middle of the street in front of our apartment complex. It was like watching a Western gunfight on TV with the gangs marching toward each other holding knives, sticks, and iron poles. I would watch the fights from our upstairs window and wonder why the police did not come until after the fights were over. I am thankful that the police respond quickly now when called, and I pray God's blessings on law enforcement.

We moved several times during my childhood, going back and forth across the state line from Kansas City, Kansas, to Kansas City, Missouri. However, I did not always change schools during these moves. At times, I was required to walk quite a distance because there was no money for bus fare, and my daddy was using our car and unavailable to take me or pick me up from school. I found walking through downtown Kansas City, Missouri very exciting; all the sights and sounds of the city were fascinating, especially the display window at one toy store. By placing a hand on the window, I was able to operate the toy locomotive that was set up in the front window of the store. Each time I walked past the store, I would try to stop and push the sign that would start the locomotive. The train would go around the track, and smoke would come out of the smokestack as the whistle blew two or three times.

Even though walking through downtown was an adventure, it was not safe. Fortunately, I always made it home safely—many times, thanks to the help of others. Sometimes, the police in Kansas City, Missouri, would give me a ride to the state line where I could then walk across the bridge into Kansas. Other times, a bus driver named Tom would see me walking and give a bus ride free of charge. Tom would let me ride to the Bottoms, which was his last stop each day; he would let me off the bus, and I would walk home from there. Then, Tom would turn his bus around and start his route all over again. I am very thankful to these people for their care.

Finding Success in Golden Gloves

We moved again during my sophomore year, and I enrolled in Bishop Ward High School where I graduated in 1969. During my last 2 years of high school, I became involved in the Golden Gloves. This program required months of training and hard work, which led me to win the 139-pound Novice Division in 1968 with an all-knockouts record. I received a Golden Gloves jacket and trophy. In 1969, I advanced to the Open Division, designed for more experienced fighters and finished runner-up in the 147-pound division. Eventually, I won a title in the 147-pound Open Division in 1972. I also had a few opportunities to compete in the National Golden Gloves, where I both won and lost fights. What a joy I experienced traveling and boxing all over the country visiting cities I never would have dreamed of seeing. I concluded with an amateur record of 67 wins, 7 defeats, and 45 knockouts. Furthermore, I received two Golden Gloves titles in the Novice Division and the Open Division and one Amateur Athletic Union (AAU) title.

Detour: Street Life and Early Marriage

In 1969, I enrolled at Kansas City Kansas Community College studying Law Enforcement for a year and a half before dropping out of school at the age of 20. In addition, I started dating a young lady and moved in with her before marriage. At this point in my life, I was not much of a Christian, although I had been baptized as an infant in the Catholic church. I did not know anything about being a Christian or the Christian rights and wrongs pertaining to marriage. We married when my girlfriend became pregnant. She was an experienced woman of the world familiar with street culture and tactics; she loved to party, drink, smoke weed, fight, and use foul language.

Her family was very dysfunctional and exhibited the same behaviors and attitude as my wife. When they were together drinking and smoking, they would get angry with one another; their disagreements would last for a long time and often escalate into physical fighting. It was not unusual for their fights to involve fists, knives, boards, tree branches, empty whiskey bottles, or whatever they could get their hands on to use as weapons. Those arguments often led to a dangerous situation in which guns were displayed,

LeRoy Green, Jr.
Age 24

and shots were fired. The shots were not aimed at anyone, just up into the air to get everyone's attention. If a person did not have a gun, they would pull out a knife or pick up whatever they could get their hands on and start swinging at everyone. Sometimes, people would be seriously hurt from stabbings or gunshots. In spite of all the chaos, the party or dice games continued as usual.

The hard thing for me was keeping my focus on what I was doing. There was so much drama happening around me that it was hard to stay focused and protect myself from harm. But when the gatherings switched from the nightclubs to my house in the West Bottoms, I decided to buy myself a pistol. I carried that pistol everywhere I went. I got a "big head," and I thought at that time that I was a big, bad dude just because I had a pistol strapped to my side.

With all the drama going on in my life, you wouldn't think that I could hold down a job working 40 hours a week. But the after-work violence did not interfere with my employment at the local fast food business of Dee's Hog House. In time, my employment at Dee's Hog House ended when Dee's was bought out by another local food chain, Go Chicken Go. By that time, I had a daughter and a son. With a family to care for, I had to find a better paying job, which I did at a roofing construction company, Sellers and Marquis.

Meanwhile, the partying and drinking continued across Kansas City, Kansas, and Kansas City, Missouri, and it became hard for me to control or keep myself from going to those gatherings. My first wife and I chose to attend most of those gatherings; drinking and dancing were our way of entertaining and enjoying ourselves. She loved gathering with family and friends to drink, smoke weed, play cards, gamble, and go to the nightclubs almost every weekend. With all that drama and excitement mingled together, the bad part of my life eventually surfaced. I ended up joining the crowd of buddies, friends, and family members drinking, smoking, cussing, fussing, and going to nightclubs.

Welcome to Adulthood

When I turned 21, I felt like I was Superman; I thought, "I can come out of my Clark Kent suit and stop hiding my drinking and my bad boy behavior. Now that I'm of legal age—an adult by law, I can drink in public and do whatever I want." To my way of thinking, I was a grown man, and no one could tell me what to do or where to go. I had my first experience with alcohol and being intoxicated on my 21st birthday. I stood up in the middle of the room and got everyone's attention. Then, I made an announcement:

"I am now 21 years old, a man." Then, I turned up a fifth of Strawberry Hill wine and drank until there was nothing left in the bottle.

The next thing I remember saying to the crowd was, "There you go. How about that?" I dropped the empty bottle on the floor as I fell back into a chair, and that is all I remember. Later that night, after the party was over and everyone had gone home, I had my first experience of what happens after you drink too much. I was very intoxicated, or you could say very drunk, to the point that I could not walk or stand up. After a while, I realized it was time for me to visit the restroom, but I could not stand up or walk because my vision was so impaired, and my legs were very weak. Guess what happen next: I ended up crawling to the restroom on my knees very slowly. I made it, and I'm sure you can guess what happened next. I stayed in the restroom most of the night, sitting on the floor next to the toilet stool.

As morning came and things got a little clearer, I said to myself in a quiet low voice, "Man, what a night, what a dramatic dangerous experience I had last night. That could have ended up a fatality any way you look at it." I made a promise to myself that I would never drink too much again, because, at that moment, I believed I had learned my lesson. I felt so humble and embarrassed by my behavior. I had foolishly consumed too much alcohol, just to prove to myself and my road buddies that I was indeed a grown man and could do whatever I wanted to do. But I was having second thoughts: Was I really a grown man?

The Ugly Truth behind the Party Lifestyle

My promise not to indulge in heavy drinking did not last; everything went wrong, and I repeated that mistake again and again. Drinking at house parties and going to nightclubs became a routine part of my life during my young adult years. Drinking and driving were part of my nightly adventures with the boys, and every weekend consisted of party days of drinking, gambling, and using foul language. Most of the people I hung out with were relatives and friends along with a few outside drinking buddies who came along with that type of entertainment during my first marriage. I definitely lived a party lifestyle during those early years—going from house to house on the weekends and sometimes after work.

Our parties were not all fun and games; they sometimes led to very serious consequences. Oftentimes, the fun and laughter of drinking and playing cards would turn into arguments among relative and friends, filled with loud, threatening talk and lots of foul language. As the party continued into the night, arguments would get more aggressive and intense until they sometimes got out of control. After dealing with this kind of behavior weekend after weekend, I started to have serious doubts about my lifestyle. All I wanted was to have fun and enjoy my drinking without arguing and fighting all the time. I knew that eventually I would have to take a break from all the clubbing, drinking, and parties. I took a good look at myself and the kinds of activity I was involved in every weekend and concluded that I could not continue this lifestyle and behavior, but old habits die hard.

I also began to realize that I had made a big mistake getting married so quickly and so young. I was not prepared for the consequences of that decision; I became convinced that marriage was not for me at that time. I had been blind to the personal part of my life and figuratively, I did not see the bus coming until I was hit head-on. I had married a woman who was also not ready for marriage; she was a pro in the worldly games. Her friends and relatives had assured her that I was a good catch, but the responsibilities of marriage were not her bag of tricks either. When I asked her, "So, what is our next step?" She merely replied, "You tell me." She was more into street time; she was an expert in worldly activities, such as parties, drinking alcohol, and sexual activities with more than one partner. I was considered a virgin when I met my first wife, and we will leave it at that. Finally, I realized that I was in the wrong place at the wrong time; I was not prepared for the baggage that came along with this marriage; I had not expected that being married would be like this—living in a war zone almost every day of the week and many weekends.

My weekend party days could have been labeled as war zones, with heavy artillery displayed from all directions, especially when weekend gatherings escalated into dangerously aggressive behavior between my wife and me. If I sponsored a party at my house that involved drinking, gambling, excessive drug use, and foul language, it could easily lead to fighting and flashing of firearms—very unstable behaviors. This behavior causes people to get out of control, and it was not my idea of having fun. Early on, I learned that I was a true freshman in this kind of behavior, dealing with the equivalent of seniors in party activity and behavior. I was totally lost and did not know what to do. But over time, I began to think that everyone acted this way, partying all the time, not showing respect for themselves and other people around them. What I'm really trying to say is that I adopted the attitude that said, "I'm having fun; if you don't like it, leave." As a young adult, I joined the crowd, and I ended up adapting to and accepting the party lifestyle because it looked okay to me. Today, that same kind of lifestyle is called being a thug or a so-called "gangster tough guy."

Playing the Role of the "Tough Guy"

I was a very bad boy at that time in my life—at least I thought I was "bad" because I bought a pistol that I could carry on my person, so I could act tough. In other words, I became a show-off. Remember, I was not in law enforcement at that time in my life. Instead, I was looking to prove myself as a grown-up tough guy. I would sit around at family gatherings or walk the streets looking for someone to say something out of the way to me—something that would give me a reason to act tough and show off my pistol. Even when I went to nightclubs, I had my pistol strapped on my side. I was all fired up, and I just wanted to be somebody important, to be noticed, and have all the attention directed toward me. Carrying a pistol gave me assurance that I was a big tough guy. I just wanted someone to run up to me or bump me the wrong way so that I would have a reason for getting angry at them for disturbing my peace; that would give me a good reason to showcase my pistol. Many times, I would sit at a table in a nightclub or bar waiting for someone to say something disrespectful toward me to disturb my peace and make me angry. In my book, that would have been justification for confronting that person(s) face-to-face and bragging about what I could or would do.

Back in the day, we so-called tough guys did a lot of talking. We would pull up our shirts or pull back our coats to showcase to everyone that "I got something [a pistol] for you if you come over this way." Of course, our words were a little harsher, if you know what I'm talking about. Looking back, I ask myself: Would I have drawn my pistol if someone had come over and challenged me? I don't know. Thank God I never found out. By putting on a showcase or a front like that, I was making a challenge to whomever.

For about 10 years, I lived a lifestyle focused on house parties, alcohol, drugs, drinking and driving, clubbing, and hanging out with the wrong people in the wrong places. I witnessed disturbances that became so aggressive that people were assaulted verbally, shot, stabbed, or badly beaten. And, truthfully, I was one of those people arguing, fussing, cussing, and fighting. Once, when I was arguing with my first wife, I was stabbed in my left hand when I tried to block a knife strike as she aimed for my face and neck. That was the only defensive move I could think of at the time; it kept her from cutting my neck. After the argument was over, the wounds in my left hand required three stitches. Other such incidents occurred many times, but thank God, no medical attention was required. However, arguments with my first wife kept getting more serious. One day, I was driving down the street with her when suddenly out of nowhere, she swung at me with a knife, aiming toward my neck. Thank God, I saw a shadow coming toward the right side of my face and moved quickly out of the way just at the right time to prevent serious injury. I got a minor cut on my arm, but that injury did not require any stitches or emergency medical attention; instead, it was taken care of at home.

After all those years of fighting, I finally decided that it was time for me to call it quits. Enough was enough! I filed for divorce to end a marriage marked by years of domestic violence at the highest level. If I had not filed for divorce, I believe that one of us or possibly both of us would have ended up seriously hurt or killed. At that time, I was not a Christian man, but I still thanked God for saving my life and getting me out of that marriage just in time with a few cuts and scratches. Even now I say, "Thank you, God; thank you, Lord."

This brings me to an end of my bad days on the streets and at home. Pausing for a moment to reflect on what happened in my life, I conclude that coming off the streets was no easy task. Our streets are man's wilderness, with no restrictions for humans or animals. I believe I made one of the best decisions of my life by coming out of man's wilderness, man's world. I realize it can only be man's world, only if man is in charge, and that keeping my friends would be impossible. Participating in the street lifestyle was like the Wild West with no law or order, no respect for each other; it was a free-for-all with every man and woman for themselves, the winner takes all.

Pause for a second and imagine yourself walking through the jungle with wildlife all around you every day of your life. Imagine that there are no restrictions, no laws, and the wild animals wander freely attacking you and everything else at will. In the real world, the animals I have just mentioned are street people who prey on other people and operate for themselves; they see, they want, and they take. We are their targets to conquer, so they can get ahead and move forward. They do not see us as friends or human beings; they see us as stepping stones. In this environment, "What would you do or what can you do?" Assuming that you have no defense and you have no weapons available to defend yourself, "Can you make it?" The answer should be yes, with prayer. This was my everyday life on the streets, and the only words that would come out of my mouth were:

Thank you, Lord for bringing me out of this wilderness, bringing me out of this jungle, bringing me off that dry dessert and saving me from a sinking ship. My Lord, my God, my Savior, you did not leave me alone! You saved me from disaster, myself, and from a life of Hell. Thank you. Thank you, Lord Amen and Amen.

Chapter 2: My Dad, the Drill Sergeant

Growing up with an Absentee Father

Growing up with my dad was not a cakewalk, nor was it as pleasant as I would have hoped to see between father and son. Occasionally, I experienced the closeness of a family in our home, but all too often, that was not the case. As I reflect on my dad's role, I must ask myself: Was he truly a father, a husband, and a friend? Of course, he had the titles, and sometimes, he did perform his duties as a father and perhaps as a husband, although only my mom could answer that question, and she is deceased. I believe that a father and son should have a close relationship, but my father was not there for me from the time I was a small child. Growing up, I longed to have a loving father-son relationship; I wanted to bond with my dad, share special conversations, and feel a unique friendship. Having those special interactions with my father would have been very important to me, but they never became a reality.

I believe that a father should be involved in his son's life as he grows up to teach him about leadership, respect, and being a friend to others. A father should teach his son the difference between right and wrong, how to be a father when he has children, and how to be a man. I did not learn these core life values from my dad; much of the time, he was simply not home when I was growing up. Oftentimes, I didn't know where he was. In other words, our family did not experience togetherness, love, friendship, and closeness the way a family should when they spend time together.

Ironically, if you had asked my dad, "How's the family?" he would probably have said something like this: "Our family is good . . . great, we are a close family, we take care of one another." Sometimes, when I rode around the city with my dad, I would hear people ask him: "How's it going, Mr. Green? How's the family?" Dad would always respond, "Everything is fine, and the family is happy and doing well." When I overheard these exchanges, I would get very upset and angry because I knew how very wrong my dad's answer was. As I think back about how life was growing up with Dad, I realize that we were not a close, peaceful, happy, and loving family.

Contrary to the way Dad portrayed us to his running buddies, we were a very distant family, and that's putting it mildly. We were separated from each other most of the time, and Dad was seldom home. We had a lot of family problems and issues growing up as kids, teenagers, and young adults, but our parents never talked about those problems. Sometimes, Mom would step in and give us some pointers and some quiet advice when dad was not around. To complicate matters, there were no adults in the home that we could go to and talk about our problems. Mom was at work all day, and no one knew Dad's whereabouts much of the time, so we had no one to talk to. If we wanted to talk to an adult, we had to wait until Mom came home from work. Often, when I tried to talk to Mom, she would push me aside, telling me to be quiet because she did not want Dad to hear our conversation.

Constant Threat of Domestic Violence

Later, I learned that Mom could not say anything or address any problems with me or the other kids while Dad was around. I could tell that Mom was very scared of Dad because every time she got the courage to stand up to Dad, things went south. My dad was mean, nasty, insulting, and bitter toward Mom and me.

Dad would fuss and yell at Mom when she brought his dinner upstairs for him to eat. Often, Dad would throw his dinner on the floor, saying he "could not eat that mess," and Mom would have to get down on her knees and clean up the "mess" or else! Too often, the arguments ended with Dad hitting Mom. I know this because I saw the evidence with my own eyes, and I heard the arguments, screams, and crying a number of times when I was supposed to be asleep. But how could I sleep when my mom was being beaten? Sometimes, I saw my mom crying because my dad beat her; I saw the bruises on her face and the tears in her eyes because she was hurting.

I tried to talk to Dad about what was going on between them. Dad's answer was, "I don't want to talk or listen to anything you have to say." He would just brush me off and tell me to go outside and play or go upstairs to my room before I got a whipping because it was none of my business. My dad's response made me so mad that I doubled up my fists to fight him; I wanted to hit him so badly that my blood was boiling. I was hot!

When Dad looked down at me and saw my fists doubled up, he said to me with a smile on his face, "Ooh, you want to fight me?" I just stood there looking up at him with a burning mad look on my face as he rocked from side to side like a boxer waiting for the bell to ring to start the fight. After seeing my reaction, Dad said: "Oh you want me, you want me, you want to fight me." And he started moving toward me with his fists balled up, accepting the challenge saying, "Come on, come on." At that moment, Mom quickly stepped in between us and told Dad, "Relax, calm down, everything is okay." So, I decided to stay in place and let my temper calm down and listen to Mom because I did not want her to get hurt anymore, trying to keep Dad and me from fighting.

I went along with Mom and decided not to make any more negative comments toward Dad or say anything about what was going on in our house that was considered family business. I knew that if I said anything to anyone about our family crisis and Dad found out about it, I would be in deep, deep trouble. My dad was vindictive—always looking to get us back or get even if he felt we had wronged him.

In public, Dad wanted to paint a picture that we were the perfect family with the perfect father and the perfect husband; the problem with that picture is that our family was far from perfect! I truly believe that Dad thought he was doing the right things to take care of his family the only way he knew how—and that meant doing things his way. But I can no longer keep silent; it's time for me to tell the truth about what my life was like growing up with Dad. First, as I have said, Dad was absent from home most of the time. None of us knew where he was, not even Mom. He would leave the house without saying anything to anybody; he would just vanish. His unexplained absences made me very frustrated and angry. My mother tried to keep peace in the family while hiding her true feelings, but I could see that she was very sad at times while Daddy was gone. When I asked Mom where Daddy was, she would usually say that he was on a boxing trip. My dad was a professional fighter, and my mother would say that he was away making money to take care of the household needs—to feed us and to take care of us.

I believed my mother's explanations for a while, but as I got older and a lot wiser, I wondered why my dad was gone so much while I was growing up. I wanted to know the truth. I finally gathered as much information as I could about my dad from my childhood years and teenage years and into my thirties, forties, and fifties. I was able to put together an honest picture of the kind of person my dad really was. It was not a pretty picture, but it's one I needed to face not only to give me peace, but also to let my brothers and sisters know about our dad and his true personality. I understand that my siblings may choose not to hear or believe what I have to say about Dad, even though it is the truth. Nevertheless, this is a story I must tell regardless of how my brothers and my sisters feel. I am tired, angry, frustrated, disappointed, embarrassed, and sad in some cases, for covering up for Dad and his actions for so many years. Right now, while I am at peace, I want to apologize to anyone who was offended, hurt, or taken advantage of by my dad over the years: I'm so sorry. I'm truly sorry.

As for my dad's whereabouts when he was absent from our family, I found out that he was not out of the city most of the time. But good old Dad was right here in the good old USA—Kansas City, Kansas, or Kansas City, Missouri, most of the time. That's right. When Daddy claimed to be out of town on boxing trips, most of the time, he was in the area; he just wasn't with us.

When my dad was home, my childhood experience was very painful, emotional, and extremely stressful because my dad could be very cruel in the way he disciplined us. Every parent knows that children need discipline: kids do the wrong things, make wrong choices, and say the wrong things without thinking before they speak. Sometimes, kids talk back to their parents, stomp their feet, and talk under their breath (murmur)—all very childish behavior. Needless to say, I got punished for doing all those things, and that was understandable to me. What troubles me so much is not that Dad punished me for something I did, but *how* he punished me. One day, for example, he punished me by whipping me with an extension cord while I was naked. As he whipped me, I started crying because all those strikes across my body with an extension cord were very, very painful. I pleaded with Daddy to stop whipping me, but he kept whipping me telling me, "Dry up those tears, or I will keep whipping you." Now, there's a catch-22! I could not stop crying because of the extreme pain of being whipped with an extension cord, but eventually the whipping stopped. However, the torture was not over. Here's the emotional part, which brings tears to my eyes even now. Daddy would get a bottle of rubbing alcohol and, without saying anything to me, he would rub me down with alcohol over those heavy, red bruises left by the extension cord across my back and other parts of my body. The burning pain was so excruciating that it made me burst out in heavy, heavy tears after the whipping.

My dad had another favorite tactic for punishing me. Sometimes, he would return home from his outings and go upstairs to his room; I would not see him until I came in from playing or from school. As soon as I closed the door, he would suddenly jump me from behind and start whipping me across my back with a belt or extension cord for something I did weeks ago. During the process, Dad kept reminding me of what I did weeks ago. He would say, "You thought I forgot, didn't you? I haven't forgotten." And he would keep whipping me, laughing all the while.

Dad loved surprising us when it came to disciplining his children. We learned to live with his spur of the moment outbursts. Dad loved putting fear into our lives, he loved putting fear in our minds, and lastly Dad loved threatening all of us, even Mom.

A Few Good Times with Dad

Despite all the problems, I did experience some good moments with Dad. Sometimes, he would take me fishing on the Kaw River, about a mile from our house. He would show me how to put a worm on my hook, throw the line out into the river, wait for the fish to bite, and then pull the fish in. But, during these times, we never talked about anything else, such as how I was doing in school or what things I was interested in—nothing. Sometimes, Dad would show me how to play baseball and how to catch a baseball. That was all good and fun for a while, until Dad would start throwing the ball back to me very hard, stinging my hand when I caught it. As I struggled catching the ball, Dad was laughing all the time, saying, "What, you can't catch the ball like me?" I answered, "I can catch the ball, see." Then, I would start crying because my dad would throw the ball back so hard that it would sting my hand as I caught it in my glove. I would say to Dad, "I don't throw as hard as you do."

Incidents like that were very disturbing; I don't understand how a dad could be so hurtful toward his children, especially me. I don't know why my dad treated us so badly. As I reflected on the past to write this book, I realized that I never heard Dad say kind words such as, "I love you" or "thank you" to me or any of my other siblings or even to my mom. That was not a side of my dad that any of us ever saw when I was growing up; it seems that he avoided such emotional expressions. Why? I don't know.

My Dad, the Showman

One thing I noticed about Dad as I was growing up is that he was a showman, and he loved to be the center of attention; in other words, it was all about him. This was very noticeable to me as I was coming along in my boxing career, especially when I was winning. Whenever I won, Dad was right there soaking up the spotlight, making comments, smiling in front of the camera, and patting me on my back saying, "This is your next champion." But his support was fleeting. When I lost a fight, where was my dad? He was not talking to the reporters or fans or even patting me on the back and saying, "We will get them next time." When I lost, Dad was a different person; he acted like a stranger to me; he was bitter, angry, and very distant from me. I discovered that part of the reason was that Dad was betting on my fights. So, when I lost a boxing match, he became angry because he had lost money. I will say this again about Dad's attitude: He loved being right and being in the spotlight as long as I was winning. But when I lost a boxing match, it was as if the spotlight had burned out on me, and where was Dad? Oh, I forgot, I lost.

As far as I can recall, Dad never accepted being wrong in his life. Dad was always right by his standards. He loved to showcase his glamour by telling his fairy tale, lifetime stories of what he had done in life and the goals he had set for himself, but no mention of his family. His attitude and behavior did not change from day one and to the day he died: he was a con man for himself.

Dad's Declining Years

In his later years, Dad was admitted to a nursing home where he could get the care he needed because his disposition was deteriorating. I don't know whether the change in Dad's attitude was caused by his medications, but in the nursing home, his attitude was hot and cold, very peaceful at times and very mean and unstable at other times. The medical staff tried to deal with Dad's attitude, but he did not like people telling him what to do. He responded by being stubborn, deceitful, ungrateful, and prideful saying, "I don't need help. I'm fine. I can take care of myself." Even at the age of 82, Dad continued disagreeing with the medical staff, telling them that he was feeling well. He said, "You can't keep me here. I can leave anytime I want to. If I can't leave, I will kill myself. If I can't do the things I want to do, there is no sense in living. I will walk away and kill myself."

When I mentioned his outbursts to the medical team, they agreed that Dad needed help. Our family decided to move forward with getting power of attorney to place him in an affordable living complex, where he could live on his own with the medical staff monitoring him to make sure he took his medications correctly. However, Dad refused to sign any papers of agreement so that he could be placed in affordable living quarters. Finally, we gave him a choice: accept this condition, or you will be put in the custody of the State of Kansas. We had a representative from the State present to confirm that process. The family's next step was to get power of attorney if Dad refused to accept the proposal. Finally, we advised Dad that the family would take action to improve his living conditions and get him the medical help he needed with or without his approval.

Dad finally agreed to the terms of the contract/agreement of the affordable living quarters in Kansas City, Kansas. My brothers and I visited the retirement complex and found it to be excellent inside and outside with a restaurant serving almost 24/7 to accommodate the retirees and their families. The entertainment was second to none; they featured class-A jazz music performances by talented individuals performing for the retirees in a wonderful atmosphere. At first, Dad enjoyed the nightclub and dinner club atmosphere, patting his feet as the music played. The entertainment was available throughout the day, with people drinking, laughing, dancing, singing, and enjoying the entertainment until—you guessed it—bedtime. Dad liked everything presented to him and agreed to the terms of the residency.

However, Dad's stay was brief. After a few weeks, my brother, who was in charge of Dad's health care and business issues, called to say that Dad was back to his old self, causing problems with staff and anyone else who wanted to help him. Dad had started complaining about everything: His bed and his room were too small, there were no big towels in the bathroom, and the restaurant did not have the food he liked to eat. He avoided having conversations with the other retirees—even with those he knew. When someone would speak to my dad, he would look at them, saying nothing, and walk away ignoring them; he was very rude. When this game plan did not work on anyone, he came up with another plan to get attention. He resorted to medical problems; he said everything was hurting—his legs, back, arms, and chest. He wanted to see a doctor, and so he got his way.

To make a long story short, we had to move Dad out of his penthouse-style living quarters, to a subdivision-type medical facility with other complaining, sick individuals all throughout the facility in wheelchairs and walkers. There was no sound of laughter, joy, or music anywhere in the facility. All I saw was the medical staff running from room to room assisting and attending to their patients who were calling for help, sometimes for no reason at all. Dad had chosen to give up penthouse-style living quarters for this. Now, he was back to his old self—arguing with everyone and using mean, foul language in all his conversations. His attitude was stubborn and negative. All I could do was to pray for Dad, asking God to help me stay focused and to take away all bitterness, meanness, and anger from my thoughts and to help Dad. I asked God to replace the evil and mean thoughts, the rage, the deceitfulness, foul language with love, kindness, goodness, and joy so that Dad could enjoy the few days he had left in peace and harmony with his family.

I went to visit Dad on March 26, 2014, and the visit went very well. We talked a little; but mostly, I listened to Dad talk about his caretakers with a vengeful attitude and bitterness. Finally, I told him that it was time for me to leave. Dad responded, "Thanks for coming by checking on me." I thought maybe Dad was changing.

Unfortunately, that was not the case. Dad had to be assigned to a specialist who dealt with special cases and behavior problems like my dad. Thank God he was getting the help he needed. But the report on Dad was not good—he continued to argue with the medical staff and caretakers, even fighting and throwing punches, trying to hit staff members. A few times, my dad succeeded in assaulting one of the staff members. After those outbreaks, Dad was put under very close observation, and he was heavily medicated, so the medical staff could focus on treating his illness. All the family could do at this time was trust God and pray that Dad would get well and come to a peaceful way of thinking and behaving. Unfortunately, that did not happen. Dad's health went from bad to worse, and the doctors advised us that there was nothing else they could do.

Dad was taken off all medications and put on the hospice floor of Research Hospital for about 30 days. On Tuesday, July 22, 2014, at about 5:00 p.m., Dad passed away. My dad had fought his last fight, and he had heard his last bell ring. In this fight, we do not yet know the decision. The decision—win or lose—will be announced by God on Judgment Day. Until then, Dad, "Rest in peace."

Chapter 3: Accepting Responsibility

I started working to earn money when I was about seven or eight years old, helping my grandmother on the weekends. Grandma paid me to do odd jobs around her house. I would wash the dinner table and chairs, making sure the chrome was shining when I finished. Then, I washed all the kitchen cabinets and dusted and polished the living room furniture. Finally, Grandma had me clean the yard all around the house; this job was more challenging than one might think. You see, the backyard was all dirt. How can you clean or sweep dirt? Well, I learned to use a broom to sweep the dirt until the yard was clean and smooth.

When I was older, I got my first "official" job at a local grocery store, stocking food shelves and the pop machine. I was also responsible for taking out the trash and sweeping and mopping the floors at closing time. I worked at that grocery store until I found a better job, working in the restaurant business with my grandma. After Grandma retired, I stayed on at the restaurant for about 12 more years.

In my mid-twenties, I decided to try a new profession, working for a construction roofing company, Sellers and Marquis. The construction job paid well, and although it was dangerous, I found the change exciting and rewarding. I was especially interested in this opportunity to learn new job skills; I saw this job change as an enjoyable adventure. As a laborer with Sellers and Marquis Roofing Company, I worked on several new complexes and buildings in the Kansas City metropolitan area, including Crown Center, Kansas City International Airport, and other buildings in Johnson and Jackson counties. Our construction team was proud to be part of the expansion in the

Kansas City metropolitan area; it gave me bragging rights. Even to this day, when I ride by Crown Center or the Kansas City airport, I always make comments, such as, "I helped put the roof on those buildings back in the day." I am very proud of the work I did on those projects. Unfortunately, the roofing job only lasted a little over a year because of work shortage, cutbacks, and layoffs.

Suddenly, I was out of work again, and I resorted to picking up aluminum cans and junk just to survive. I applied for a job with Wells Fargo Security Company to work as an armed security officer at Columbia Steel in the Kansas City, Missouri, stockyards. My application was accepted, and I worked at that job for a little over a year. Then, I had to live on unemployment for several months, until I received a call from a friend who was a boxing promoter. He knew that I was looking for work and asked if I would be interested in another job as an armed security guard. I was grateful for the opportunity, and I was even more excited when he told that I was being considered for a security position with the Kansas City Chiefs professional football team at Arrowhead Stadium. Wow! Who would have guessed that I might have a chance to work for the Kansas City Chiefs. The security director scheduled my interview with the owner of the Chiefs.

Prior to being considered for the job with the Chiefs, I had fought boxing matches in the Kansas City metropolitan area as well as other US and international locations such as Topeka, St. Louis, Las Vegas, New York, New Jersey, Chicago, California, Canada, and Italy. My professional boxing career record was 15 wins and 7 defeats; 11 of my wins were by knockout. My wins included the 1978 Midwest Middleweight Championship, which I won with a 7-round Technical Knockout (TKO) over veteran fighter Johnny Heard from Chicago—not bad. As a professional boxer, I met some of the legendary champions as well as two top boxing promoters. I also had a professional career in martial arts, winning four kickboxing exhibition bouts by TKO. I was surprised to learn that one of my opponents was a brown belt in martial arts, which is just one step below a black belt.

By the time I interviewed with the owner of the Kansas City Chiefs and his hiring personnel, I had established myself as a professional boxer, but I had no idea that they knew all about me from my boxing career. After my interview, I was hired by the Kansas City Chiefs as a security guard working

106 Amateur Fights
66 KOs   Lost 5

18 Pro Fights
10 KOs   Won 12

World's Middleweight Contender
LEROY GREEN

at Arrowhead Stadium and other Kansas City Chiefs' property. My role as security guard was very rewarding, especially since it allowed me to meet some well-known NFL football players. Typically, I would watch the Kansas City Chiefs' daily practice and their workouts inside and outside the facility, and I would also interact with players in the workout room during my workouts. I was still a professional fighter, and I kept myself in shape working out in the weight room and running around the stadium after my scheduled work hours.

During my workouts, some of the football players would watch me go through my boxing workouts, and one day, they asked, "How would you fight or handle big guys like us?" Before I could answer, one of the big guys stretched out his arms as if he were throwing a punch at me, putting his hand on the top of my head and said, "What can you do with that? How can you handle that?"

I said, "Wow." With his arms stretched out, it looked like I was standing a mile away. I calmly answered the football player, "You have a pretty good arm reach. It would be kind of hard for me to get inside and hit you." So, this football player said again, "Come on, hit me. Let me see what you can do. Show me something." Because of his height and reach, the only counter-move I could do was to throw a right-hand uppercut strike, directly under his elbow where it was extended to the fullest. I gave him a small tap on his elbow and explained to him, "If I go all out and hit your elbow with full force, your elbow would be broken or dislocated." As I continued throwing light punches toward his head, elbow, and body, the player concluded that I was pretty good. I added, "In truth, with a guy your size, I would not have much of a chance. At best, I might do a small amount of damage." I was a little guy, five feet eleven, trying to hit a great big guy, six feet eight or nine, whose body was built to take hard blows.

After our conversation, we ended up doing a little comic routine for some of his teammates. Our routine showcased this big football player putting his hand on the top of my head while I jumped up and tried to hit him on his chin. Remember, this football player was six feet nine. Of course, I could not hit this big guy because he was too tall, and I could not reach him. But through it all, I had lots of fun with him and other Chiefs players. I enjoyed our conversations, and sometimes, I showed them boxing moves they could use to get their opponents off-balance during their football games. For instance, if a football player adjusted his body movements to match up with his hands and feet, his whole body would work together as one unit, moving from side to side. Using this type of movement, he could distract his opponent, keeping him confused and off-balance. Over my three-and-a-half-year tenure with the Kansas City Chiefs, I enjoyed the connections and fellowship I had with some of the players; I am very thankful to the Chiefs for that opportunity. At this point in my career, I was ready for a change and I decided to leave security work and move into law enforcement.

Chapter 4: Joining the Big League

Leaving security work and moving into law enforcement was like going from the minor league to the major league. I went to the Kansas City, Kansas Police Department to apply for a position. At the Personnel Office, I was informed that the Personnel Director was not hiring at that time, and I was directed to the Wyandotte County Sheriff's Office, which was hiring. I was hired by the Sheriff's Office after a lengthy debate with the hiring administrator about my job title and duties. Initially, I wanted to apply for a position as a patrol officer, but the administrator kept changing the wording on my application from *patrolman* to *jailor*. This little game went on and on until I finally accepted the jailor position.

Working as a jailor taught me a lot about people. I also learned a lot about honesty, fairness, and integrity because I saw firsthand how the deputies treated the inmates. I also saw how the inmates treated the deputies. There were no winners in this situation; neither side liked or respected the other. Why? Because there was so much foul language, meanness, bitterness, and deceit. Both sides made threats, wanting to do harm to each other and their families. From what I saw and heard early on, I had to ask myself, "Which party belonged in jail—the inmates or the deputies?" I decided, "Both." I wanted to do something to ease the tension and bitterness and restore peace to both sides, but I did not dare intervene because I was a new employee and a freshman in this line of work. I did not want to make a bad situation worse.

I got my own test soon enough. While doing rounds in the jail one day, an inmate confronted me saying, "Hey, Green, everybody is scared of you because you are a boxer." He added, "I am not scared of you. I will kick your ass!"

When he said that, it disturbed me greatly, so I called for a guard to open the gate because I wanted to get inside this inmate's cell and kick his rear end. I did not move from my original spot; I stood right in front of his cell starring at him until the guard arrived to open his cell door. I looked the inmate straight in the eye and said, "Let me see how tough you are when the guard opens this gate because I'm going to show you what I can do." The inmate countered, "What you going to do?" Without really thinking, I said, "I'm going to come inside your cell, and I'm going to knock you out." As I turned to tell the deputy to let me in this inmate's cell, the inmate quickly said, "Hey, Green, that's all right. I was just testing you. I did not know you were that serious about your job. I thought you were weak like some of the other guards." I said, "Look, man, I come to work every day to do my job, showing you and everyone else in here that I am not a judge or a jury. I call you 'Sir' because I don't know your name. To get respect, you have to give respect." A strange thing happened after that incident in the jail. I believe the news about that confrontation got around to the other inmates. After that incident, all the inmates started calling me "Mr. Green" or "Officer Green." That's when I knew I had earned the inmates' respect—all because of one incident with an inmate. After that encounter, I had no more problems during my tour of duty working in the jail.

I didn't understand why the other shifts continued to have problems dealing with inmates fighting about their commissary, visitations, break times, feeding time, and cleanup time. I asked the captain and the warden if I could help, by talking with the inmates to identify the problems that disrupted their daily activities. The warden gave me permission to talk with the inmates to pinpoint the problems that were causing friction between the inmates and the officers. My investigation revealed that one shift of officers was causing most of the problems among the inmates after hours; they were showing favoritism toward certain inmates, including the female inmates who promised favors to the officers. All those issues were addressed with the warden who contacted the district attorney. Some inmates were charged with soliciting the deputies, which caused those deputies to turn in their resignations for accepting inmate solicitations.

After those problems were cleaned up, the jail became a peaceful place to work. I was pleased to see everyone working together to bringing back respect and honesty to the Sheriff's Office. There were rumors that one inmate wanted to challenge me, but that turned out to be a false alarm. The inmate in question had positive things to say—he told the other inmates, "That Green will treat you good and will find a way to help you with your personal and court problems. He's okay." When the warden shared these comments with me, I was very pleased. My tour of duty working in the jail wound down as I got training in other areas of corrections. With this experience under my belt, it was time for me to move on to a more rewarding position within the Sheriff's Office—Road Patrol was my choice.

I sent my transfer request to the classification office, expecting that it would be processed smoothly. That did not happen. Once again, the position on my paperwork was changed—this time, from *road patrol* back to *jailor*. I was stunned. I asked who had changed my transfer papers, but no one could give me any information about the change on my transfer request. I retrieved my transfer papers and verified that they had indeed been changed. I was very upset and angry. I decided to change my transfer papers back to the original order and returned the transfer papers to the front office.

The same thing happened again. This time, I dug a little deeper and a little wider, and I found the person responsible for changing the job title on my transfer request. It shouldn't have come as a surprise: the guilty party was the classification officer who had changed my original application. This was my first sign of discrimination within the Sheriff's Office. So, I went to the Captain and explained that I had filled out an application for transfer to Road Patrol. I told him that I felt it was time for me to advance in my career as a law enforcement officer, and I also explained the problems I had with my application. So, the Captain decided to deliver my application for transfer in person, and he ordered the classification officer to process the application at once. I was transferred to Road Patrol, and my career in law enforcement moved on to the next level. This incident was my first experience with racial discrimination within the Wyandotte County Sheriff's Office. After doing some investigation on my own and talking to some of the senior deputies, I learned that there were no black patrol deputies as far as we could determine. The senior deputies said that I would be the first certified African American Road Patrol Deputy in the Sheriff's Office. I paused for a moment and said to myself, "Oh well." But in reality, I had no idea what was waiting for me down the road.

I finally began my duties as a Road Patrol Officer and, for the most part, everything started well. I was assigned a training officer who taught me the dos and don'ts, how to fill out reports, and issue citations. I was trained on all the road patrol equipment, such as the speed radar gun, the DUI machine for intoxicated driver arrests, and other equipment used for road patrol procedures. To become certified as a law enforcement officer, I went to the Law Enforcement Academy in Hutchinson, Kansas, for their 12-week program. I graduated with honors and was ready to fulfill my duties as a Road Patrol Officer for the Wyandotte County Sheriff's Office. I felt very proud of this accomplishment; I was excited to be a professional law enforcement officer.

As I continued my patrol duties, I noticed that some of the deputies' attitudes toward me started to change, but I didn't know why. Then, I experienced an unforgettable incident on the job. When I was ordered to partner with one of the senior patrol deputies, everything went well for quite a while. I learned a lot from this senior deputy, but one day, our partnership changed drastically. While on patrol in Wyandotte County, I was talking with my supervisor when he suddenly said to me, "LeRoy, I like you, you are all right. You're not like those other niggers." That shocked me, and I froze in my tracks. I was speechless and confused. He kept talking, not realizing that he had just made a racial slur toward me. He went on to say, "Those other niggers, they—" Then, there was a pause, and he looked at me with a frightened, pale look on his face realizing what he had just said to me, an African American, a black male. This supervisor's next words were, "LeRoy I am sorry, I'm so sorry." He said, "I wasn't talking about you; you're not like those other—." He stopped and said, "You're different." My response to him after his comment was, "That's okay. You just said what was on your mind. I am not upset or mad." Almost every day after that incident, he kept apologizing and buying me gifts, saying that he felt bad. I refused to take the gifts and assured him that everything was okay. He continued this behavior until the day he died.

Another disturbing incident happened with a different supervisor who always wanted to show me off to the other deputies and officers from the neighboring departments. Sometimes, he would call me off my patrol duties and ask me to meet him at a local coffee shop out in the county. When I arrived for our meeting, he would have two or three white officers from other police departments in Wyandotte County with him. I would go inside and ask my supervisor what he needed me to do, and he would tell me to take a break and have a cup of coffee. I would say, "That's okay, sir. I'm fine. I'm still on patrol." He would respond, "I'm your supervisor, and I said sit down and have a cup of coffee. Everything is okay." So, I would have a cup of coffee. Here's the catch: my supervisor wanted to show off in front of the other officers with him, letting them know that he was in charge. This supervisor would give me instructions about how to stop vehicles and issue citations, search houses, and make neighborhood checks even though I already knew these procedures. After the coffee break and his training session with me were over, he said very loudly so that all the other patrons in the café could hear, "Now, you can go back on patrol." For a while I believed that he was following me when I transported arrestees to the Wyandotte County jail. I frequently saw his vehicle at the same location when I was returning to my patrol district from the Wyandotte Jail. A little investigation revealed that he was not following me, but he was going home to sleep—yes, going home to sleep during his shift. Several times, I also caught the same supervisor sleeping in his patrol car parked in the annex. After several people reported him to the sheriff and undersheriff, my supervisor was replaced.

The supervisor who replaced him had even more disturbing behavior issues. The new supervisor not only slept in his patrol car, but he consumed alcohol regularly on the job while operating a county-owned vehicle. This supervisor hid his alcohol in a black canteen he carried with him every day in his patrol car; he regularly got very intoxicated on the job, causing a lot of confusion among our law enforcement agencies and our deputies. Ironically, most of our senior deputies, supervisors, and even officers from other departments knew of this problem, but they said nothing. Finally, the sheriff and undersheriff became aware of my supervisor's drinking problem and, after an intensive investigation, this supervisor was first suspended and later terminated. Afterward, our department was once again a relaxed and peaceful operation where deputies could perform their duties as professionals.

Chapter 5: Breaking the Color Barrier

After peace was restored at the annex and patrol returned to normal duties, I was transferred to the front office and put in charge of a new program called Tag Enforcement. The sheriff and undersheriff designed this program to go after people who lived in Wyandotte County, Kansas, but had out-of-state license plates on their vehicles. Kansas State Statutes 8-142/8-127 require that residents of Kansas City, Kansas, and Wyandotte County must register their vehicles in the county unless they have a legal excuse that exempts them from this requirement.

The Tag Enforcement program started well, although there was dissent from some residents and business owners. In certain areas, I had my share of confrontations with residents, business owners, clergy, and other taxpayers as I sought to enforce the statutes. I found myself having to justify my duties, explaining that I was simply doing my job as a Wyandotte County law enforcement officer. In certain parts of the county, residents questioned my identity. Although I wore a proper uniform and had a badge attached to my shirt and sheriff's patches on my sleeves, some residents seemed to doubt my identity or my authority to do the job. Their first response was often, "Who are you?" I would show my sheriff department photo ID and state that I was Wyandotte County Sheriff Deputy Green in charge of the Wyandotte County Tag Enforcement unit. I informed them that I was investigating a complaint submitted to the Sheriff's Office. Often, the complaining party would call the Kansas City, Kansas Police Department or the Sheriff's Office to verify my identity, asking whether the department had an officer in the area checking license plates. Questions about my identity always came from individuals who were not African American. In time, I realized that racial discrimination was a factor in some of my experiences as the Tag Enforcement officer. Some days were very emotional and upsetting to me, but I learned to pause, take a deep breath, relax, and ask God to help me through those troublesome times. God always sent an answer to me by the Holy Spirit to help me respond to each challenge, even though some of the complaints were very disrespectful not only to me, but to other races as well.

Finally, the sheriff issued an order to investigate the complaints filed by individuals whose residency in Wyandotte County, Kansas, was in question. Fortunately, his investigation confirmed that the individuals who had filed complaints were indeed in violation of statutes 8-127/8-142. With proper enforcement, this program brought in millions of dollars of tax revenue to the county that would otherwise have been lost. After 5 years supervising the Tag Enforcement program, I was promoted to Sergeant. The Sheriff's Office continued to conduct traffic checks across Kansas City, Kansas, and Wyandotte County, with assistance from most, if not all, our law enforcement agencies, which included the Kansas State Troopers and the Kansas City, Missouri Police Department for traffic checks on both sides of the state line between Kansas and Missouri.

In 1995, a new sheriff was elected, and he asked me to be his undersheriff. At first, I was puzzled by his offer as he told me that I was not the first person he asked to be his undersheriff. The sheriff said that the other individuals he'd asked had declined his offer. But he said that my name kept coming up in conversations all around the county as the top candidate to be undersheriff. I was speechless and shocked, so the sheriff said, "Well, what's your answer?" I said, "Yes, okay." With that, I became the second African American undersheriff in Wyandotte County. I had no idea that this would mark a significant moment in Kansas history and the start of a political and racial fight that spanned my career. I accepted the sheriff's offer in a private meeting with just the two of us. In that meeting, the sheriff advised me that he was putting me in charge of the Sheriff's Office because I was more knowledgeable about the sheriff's duties and responsibilities than he was since he came from the Kansas City, Kansas Police Department. The sheriff requested that I check with him before making any changes or decisions regarding the structure and policies of the Sheriff's

Office. I thought that was very professional and honest, and he earned my respect from then on. The sheriff and I had a very good working relationship during his tour of duty. I could not have asked for a better sheriff or boss.

While I was the undersheriff, several areas of the Sheriff's Office were upgraded. First, we upgraded our manpower and then our Tag Enforcement unit so that our deputies would receive up-to-date training and be more professional in dealing with the public. Next, we increased our manpower in all areas of the Sheriff's Office, especially our Tag Enforcement unit as we continued to go after people who refused to register their vehicles in Wyandotte County, Kansas. The Sheriff's Office also put together a Fugitive Apprehension unit to pursue individuals who had outstanding federal, county, or city warrants. A number of fugitives were arrested through our Tag Enforcement program and our warrant division as we worked with other agencies.

After a little over 3 years working with the new sheriff, I was pleased that the Sheriff's Office was operating very professionally. But I should have known that was not the time to relax—everything was about to change! The sheriff called me into his office and said, point blank, "I am resigning. I have completed all I wanted to do, so I am turning everything over to you. Are you okay with that?" I said, "I heard you." Then, I was speechless—I froze. This was similar to our talk when he offered me the undersheriff position. The sheriff asked me again, "What's your answer?" By law, the Kansas State Statute says, when the current sheriff leaves office for any reason, the undersheriff assumes the title of sheriff finishing out the current sheriff's tour of duty until the next election, at which time a new sheriff will be elected. Therefore, I assumed the position of sheriff and was sworn in by one of the district court judges to finish out the 3 years left in the sheriff's term.

At that moment, I became the first African American sheriff not only in Wyandotte County, but also in the State of Kansas. A historic breakthrough was recorded on that day; thank you, Lord. For the first 6 months to a year, my tenure as sheriff had a calm, routine atmosphere, from the front office to the jail to the road patrol. Then, the situation exploded, and everything started to fall apart. First, the jail population increased dramatically because the Kansas City, Kansas Police Department decided to arrest anyone who was in violation of the law—I mean everyone. This increased the population of the

Wyandotte County jail and created a serious shortage of manpower to keep up with the demand. Furthermore, the increased jail population caused financial and budget problems, and I began to get tremendous pressure from the jail population control committee, wanting answers as to why the jail was so overcrowded. All areas of the city-county unified government were pressuring me to come up with a solution that would decrease overcrowding in the jail.

I explained to the jail population control committee that the increase in population was due to a significant change in the Kansas City, Kansas Police Department's patrol and arrest procedures, arresting anyone in violation of the law, no matter what level of violation. Some government officials wanted me to change the way the Wyandotte County jail and the Sheriff's Office operated; they wanted to dictate how I operated the jail and the Sheriff's Office. Specifically, they proposed that we take all our deputies off the street and assign them to the jail to ease the shortage of manpower in the jail. Second, they wanted to turn all law enforcement duties over to the Kansas City, Kansas Police Department and privatize the Wyandotte County jail. Those moves would have left the Sheriff's Office with only a few deputies, all assigned to the front office and responsible only for securing the district courts and handling process serving. These changes would have left the Sheriff's Office with no law enforcement duties. As sheriff, I refused to implement these changes.

So, the fight with officials at all levels of the unified government was on, and those officials summoned the Wyandotte County Sheriff's Office to federal court, in an attempt to take control of the Wyandotte County jail. When I received the summons to appear in federal court, I did not know what to do. I was shaken, frightened, and extremely nervous because I was going up against the mighty and powerful unified government. The only thing I could think of was prayer, so I went to God in prayer. As I was praying, the Holy Spirit whispered to me saying, "Look at Psalm 23:4–6":

Yea, though I walk through the valley of the shadow of death, I will fear no evil; for you are with me; Your rod and Your staff, they comfort me. You prepare a table before me in the presence of my enemies; you anoint my head with oil; my cup runs over. Surely goodness and mercy shall follow me all the days of my life; and I will dwell in the house of the LORD Forever.

That word from God gave me strength and courage to stand up and testify to the federal judge concerning my side of the story and my authority as sheriff of Wyandotte County, Kansas. After the judge heard both sides, he looked over at the members of the unified government and said, "Gentlemen, the sheriff is his own boss. He is in control of the jail and all other functions of the Sheriff's Office. The sheriff answers to no one so long as the sheriff stays within the state statutes of the State of Kansas, this is my ruling." The unified government lost its appeal in federal court, and the operation of the Wyandotte County jail remained in the authority of the Sheriff of Wyandotte County, Kansas City, Kansas, LeRoy Green Jr. by order of Kansas State Statute, which states that "the elected sheriffs of said counties in the State of Kansas will be in charge of their county jail in his or her jurisdiction." This ruling applied across the State of Kansas—all 105 counties—ruling that the sheriff will remain in authority over the county jail. Thank you, my Lord. You were with us all the way. May God be the glory.

Chapter 6: My Trips Overseas— South Africa and South Korea

Before I share about my overseas adventures to South Africa and South Korea, I want to give thanks to my God because without God, these trips would never have happened. These trips were the most exciting adventures of my life other than accepting Christ as my Lord and Savior. What joy I had meeting and exchanging values and testimonies with people from other cultures across the world. In just a short time, I developed a truly amazing and precious friendship, which I will describe later in this chapter.

Experiencing South Africa

I had a rare opportunity to travel to South Africa as part of a delegation of law enforcement officers. I found the South African people to be heartwarming, kind, respectful, and cheerful. They always greeted us with a smile. Their attitude was positive even though some areas of the country were experiencing significant rates of crime, poverty, homelessness, and a major outbreak of AIDS. With such pressing issues, one might think South Africans would be sad and downcast, but they still managed to have a smile on their faces and joy in their hearts.

Our visit began in Johannesburg when we checked into the Sandton Crowne Plaza Hotel, which I was told was one of the finest hotels in South Africa. I felt like a king, checking into this palace with its marble floors, gold trim, elegant pictures on the walls, and gold-plated bathrooms and showers. I could hardly believe I was staying in a hotel of such high quality with service provided around the clock by gracious staff members. Our delegation consisted of two sheriffs and eight police chiefs. When we toured local police stations, the Magistrates Courts, and the business areas, I was surprised to see the South Africans approach the

sheriffs and engage in conversations with us before they talked with the rest of our delegation. I was told that they approached the sheriffs first because they knew about and respected the office and position of sheriff. In South Africa, the position of sheriff has a long history of law enforcement authority, dating back to the sixteenth century.

After some preliminary activities, we began to discuss law enforcement business with the South African police chiefs from Johannesburg and Cape Town. As we talked about police matters, I concluded that South Africa had changed greatly since apartheid had been abolished. The new government seemed sincerely committed to changing the way they operate for the betterment of the people—not for white or black, not for rich or poor, but for all people to be united as one with equal rights. I congratulated the police chiefs and prosecutors for continuing to change the laws not only to prosecute criminals, but also to rehabilitate inmates by creating programs that reduce the number of repeat offenders. I was very impressed with the progress that the South African government had made in the communities, establishing neighborhood watch groups that work alongside faith-based ministries. Speaking to the South African police delegation, I said, "In order for any program to work, you must involve everyone and then trust in your faith in God, and you will see that God will allow those programs to happen. Although you will have some negative reviews and uprisings, you will also experience more joy, peace, and happiness in your fight against crime by doing what is right and what is honest." After our session, the Director of Social Service thanked me for including God in the process.

Next, we stayed overnight at Kruger National Park and toured the wildlife the following morning. Our residence and sleeping quarters were on the reservation at the Kruger Gate Hotel. I had the extraordinary experience of eating wildlife cooked to perfection over an open fire in the jungle while a lion named Mustafa lurked in the background behind a huge fence that surrounded our hotel. The game warden gave us strict orders not to wander outside at night because Mustafa liked to roam around the camp at night. Mustafa's presence also explained why the game warden carried a big rifle. This lion, which was still young and playful, accompanied us on our elephant walk the next morning. As the group walked along the trail, the lion would walk between our legs, bumping our legs one after another. The game warden told us that the lion did

this to test us—to see who was strong and who was weak. The game warden instructed us to stay close together because the lion would occasionally jump up on someone in the group in a playful jester trying to knock that person to the ground, which could result in injuries.

With God's blessing, I had this extraordinary experience of walking among wild animals in their jungle setting. At first, I couldn't believe that I was in the midst of the jungle just like the shows I had watched on *Wild Kingdom*. Only, I was seeing the animals in real life, not on television or in a magazine. I saw lions, elephants, rhinos, zebras, tigers, leopards, water buffalos, water hogs, a mean bull elephant, monkeys, all kind of birds, ducks, and other water fowl. At one point, a herd of elephants that had been out all day decided to go on a charging rampage. In jest, I told our safari group, "I can see the headlines now: 'Sheriff of Wyandotte County, Kansas, attending a law enforcement delegation program in South Africa, was trampled by a bull elephant and eaten by a pack of lions.'" Suddenly, the situation became dangerous. The game warden came over to the group and said in a very soft voice, "It's time for us to leave this area very quickly and at the same time." Meanwhile, the game warden loaded two big rounds in his gun. I said, "Bye."

Next, our group was taken on a night ride through the jungle. Just as we got started, we came upon two lions—a male and a female. As we stayed hidden from the lions, I watched the female courting and teasing her male counterpart, but the male seemed not to be interested in the female's courting efforts. After a while, the game warden said that we had seen enough, and he turned the jeep around to head back. Suddenly, the jeep hit a huge termite hole. Everyone stopped talking and looked at each other as if to say, "What do we do now?" The front wheel of the jeep was completely buried up to the bumper—I mean gone! Our driver tried to drive out of the hole without any success. Then, we realized that one of our passengers had been thrown from the jeep when we hit the termite hole. We determined that the passenger was all right and got her back into the jeep. Just then, the game warden told us to stay in the jeep and not make any sudden moves or loud noises that might draw attention from the lions that were only about 25 feet away. I thank God that the lions were still courting and not paying us any attention. Thank you, Lord again. Help finally arrived and we returned to our hotel safely. Thank you, Lord, one more time.

From Johannesburg, we traveled to Cape Town, which is a magnificently beautiful city surrounded by mountains, and a remarkable ocean vista. The city spread out before us like a scene you might see in a story book—soaring mountains, beautiful homes, stores and quaint shops, restaurants, and shopping centers. I had a chance to explore Cape Town and experience it in ways I will never forget. First, I jogged on the boardwalk for a nice little run. As I did so, I noticed just how peaceful and quiet it was except for the beautiful waves coming in from the ocean. I stopped and listened to the penguins on the shore, chattering and chasing each other, having fun like at a family reunion. Another exciting adventure was touring Table Mountain, which we accessed by cable car. I had never ridden in a cable car before. The cable car went very high in the air going from mountain to mountain held by one cable that swayed from side to side; I sat quiet as a mouse and still as a statue on the ride to the top of Table Mountain. When we finally reached the mountaintop, I was not prepared for what I saw. I commented to our group, "I feel like I'm in heaven looking down to earth." It was one of the most beautiful sights I have ever seen; we could see all of Cape Town, the ocean, and the smaller mountains—all so quiet, peaceful, and beautiful. I felt like I was looking out of a window from heaven down upon God's creation; it was breathtaking.

God's Call to Witness in South Africa

I came to understand that the real reason for my trip to South Africa was for me to witness to others about the truth of God. His call for me to witness began at the very start of this amazing opportunity for me to travel overseas. As I sat in New York's Kennedy Airport waiting for our flight to Johannesburg, a young woman approached me saying, "Good morning." I replied, "Good morning to you as well." As she continued to make conversation, I detected that she was from another country. She asked, "Are you from New York?" I replied, "No, ma'am. I am from the State of Kansas." She asked where I was going, and I replied, "Johannesburg, South Africa." She asked how I happened to be going to South Africa; I told her that it was a spiritual gift from God that made this trip possible for me. Her next words were, "Wow, I can't believe it. I'm here in another country where I met a man, a Christian man." I said to her, "Whatever you do, trust and keep your faith in God." She assured me she would do that.

My next encounter was with a couple on the plane during a stopover in South Africa. The conversation began with introductions; they were from Pakistan, and I introduced myself as a member of a US law enforcement delegation headed to South Africa. The couple responded, "South Africa is a beautiful place. You will enjoy it there." I smiled and said, "I hope I don't get eaten by the animals." They assured me that the animals are fine, but the wife said, "The streets of New York are more dangerous than the animals in the jungle." I said, "Wow, you know what, you're right because when God created man and all the animals in the Garden of Eden, there was peace, joy, and no sin." I advised the couple not to get too comfortable because here's the fallout. In the Garden of Eden, Satan tempted man to eat fruit from a particular tree, which God had given Adam strict orders not to eat (Genesis 3). From Adam's disobedience, sin came into the world, and everything changed; now, we are dealing with Adam's sin in our society today.

After we arrived in South Africa, my next opportunity to spread the Word of God came with our bus driver who by chance had dinner with our tour group one evening. He sat at my table along with two other delegates. The conversation among our group was sparked after the two delegates prayed and blessed the food we were about to eat. I commended them for praying before the meal. I believe that prayer is for everyone without discrimination or prejudice. Then, the bus driver opened up and told us that his name was Moses. He testified that he used to be bitter and jealous because he did not have the things that other people had. He said, "I wanted new clothes, money, a new car, and a new house along with the joy and happiness that other people were experiencing." He said that his mother was always praying and taking care of the family. In time, he found God. He got a new job, and now he can go out and buy anything and everything he wants. He thanked God and said, "I'm not bitter anymore, I love everyone." My response was this:

I am happy for your newfound freedom with God, and I am happy for all that God has given you. All that you have right now was there all the time. God was just waiting for you to change your attitude and behavior and come to Him. First of all, there was a process that God wanted you to go through—the process of forgiveness. Without forgiveness, you would still be standing at the door knocking, waiting for your blessings. Since you found God and released your anger and bitterness and forgave those who had offended you, God has a blessing for you, and that's when God will open the doors to your newfound treasures. As long as you keep faith and trust in God, God will continue to send blessings your way. Amen.

My next opportunity to spread the word came at a dinner hosted for our delegation by a South African family, who were the organizers of the People to People Ambassador Program. During the welcome session, while everyone was getting to know each other, I was going around the room shaking hands. I met the organizer of the program, who asked, "What led you to come to South Africa, what was your motivation?"

I replied, "My name was selected from a group of people. Why? I don't know. But speaking from a spiritual level, God made this trip possible." The organizer responded, "It's funny you say that because I have a mission that I operate to help feed the hungry and help the needy, and right now I'm looking for a bigger building where I could feed more people. We may have to close down the mission because there is not enough room or food to keep up with all the people who are coming to the mission to be fed." I asked, "Remember the time in the Bible when Christ fed the multitude of people with just a few fish and a few loaves of bread?" He said yes, and I responded, "Don't worry. Everything will be all right."

While we were eating dinner, an extraordinary thing happened. The organizer stood up and got the attention of the delegation saying, "I have some good news to tell everyone. We don't have to close the mission after all. I just received a phone call from a company that has a building big enough to accommodate and feed more people, and they will give the building to us for the mission. Hold on, there's more. The company will supply all the food that is needed to keep our mission open. I don't have to close down the mission after all." Then, the organizer looked over at me and said, "Thank you, sheriff, for those spiritual words of confidence. God did it." At that moment, I knew why I had been chosen to make this trip to Africa—I was to deliver a message from God. Amen. I said to the director:

> **We don't know why certain events happen or why some people are hungry and some people have plenty. All we have to do is keep doing God's work, helping and praying for those who are in need. Furthermore, there are several stories in the Bible that show the goodness of God, the healing power that can mend a broken heart and heal the sick.**

The director said, "Sheriff you were destined to be here at this time. God made this trip possible at this time for you to be here talking to me." I said, "Sir, you just confirmed my trip to South Africa to me. It was worth it to have an opportunity to witness to people across the globe. God is a wonderful God." I paused and said:

> *Thank you, Lord, for giving me the opportunity to travel to another country and talk about the goodness of God. South Africa is known for racism and civil rights violations. On day one, you could not have told me that I would be standing in the living room of a white family in Johannesburg, South Africa, having a conversation about the goodness of God. Amen.*

Challenge of Crime and Poverty

Finally, our law enforcement command staff met with the police chiefs of South Africa to asked questions about the crime rate in South Africa, compared with that of the United States. Unfortunately, the number of crimes was increasing every year; murders, for example, were up about 2,500 a year. I rode with local police officers on night patrol in one of the worse cities in South Africa. The city was infested with malaria, AIDS, and a high rate of crime. Living conditions were the worst I have seen; it was a very sad scene. Many of the people live in shacks and tents like those shown in the *Tarzan* movies; the houses are made from pieces of tin, wood, plastic, old doors, tires, pieces of iron, and metal. There was no electricity and running water, so the people must walk for miles carrying buckets or jugs on their shoulders supported by a stick across their backs to collect water and then bring it back home. Each toilet facility was a box inside a shed, like our old-time outhouses. These self-made toilets were in a field directly behind each person's shack; these toilets were no more than a hole in the ground surrounded by a box made of wood painted black for identification.

Next, we went into the crime-infested area of the city, which was overrun by local gangs, drug dealers, prostitutes, and con men and women. There was also an area where sex predators hung out, promoting their products. Nearby, we saw food vendors on the street corners or wherever they found a vacant spot to set up and sell their products. They had open fires going with pots boiling so they could cook food right on the street corners. I was told not to ask anyone what they were cooking, but I did. I asked one of the vendors, "What you cooking, buddy?" He said, "Good food, man. Good food. You would like it, man." I asked again, "What are you cooking?" He said, "Hold on man—sheep heads, man." I said, "Beg your pardon. You said you are cooking what?" He said, "Sheep heads, man." That was all we needed to hear; that was enough for the members of our delegation who overheard this exchange. We huddled together and agreed it was time for us to leave this part of the city.

It was almost time for us leave South Africa, and the South African delegation and other citizens hosted a wonderful farewell dinner for us. I learned a lot from the South Africans I met. I appreciated the value they place on helping others before they help themselves. I believe that attitude is one of the reasons many South Africans put their faith in Almighty God, believing the more they give, the more they will receive. My trip to South Africa was a tremendous learning experience. Thank you, Lord. Amen.

Experiencing South Korea

My connection with South Korea began long before I traveled to the country. Let me go back a few years to the beginning of a very special friendship. My friend is a pastor from South Korea who owns businesses in Kansas City, Kansas, and Kansas City, Missouri. At the beginning, I had no idea that our relationship would lead to a blessing set up by God. I met my friend from Korea while I was undersheriff when I interviewed ministers who wanted to bring spiritual teaching to the Wyandotte County jail inmates. Spiritual teaching in the jail was acceptable if the ministers and their small congregations operate within the guidelines of Christian ministries and the Sheriff's Office Policy. Some ministries complied with the guidelines, but others deviated from the guidelines, bringing in their own worship idols. Those who deviated from guidelines were dismissed from the program.

My Korean friend and others who were approved operated very good programs set up to help individuals who lacked jobs, education, or spiritual background. Those groups also helped individuals who had issues with law enforcement, such as warrants for traffic tickets or other misdemeanors. Several businesses in Wyandotte County, Kansas, and Jackson County, Missouri, helped individuals find employment and assistance from the district attorney's office. As my friend and I worked together on programs across Wyandotte County and other areas in Kansas and Missouri, our friendship grew stronger.

I was surprised when my friend invited me to accompany him on a business trip to South Korea. Initially I hesitated, not sure I was ready for this, but I accepted his invitation, and we were off to South Korea. I learned a lot from my friend about South Korea from educational, cultural, spiritual, and Christian perspectives. When we arrived in South Korea, we were met at the airport by a large gathering of government and law enforcement dignitaries. My friend was just as surprised as I was to see the gathering of so many government officials and citizens. My friend had no idea that we would be met with such honor, so he left me for a few moments to see what was going on. When he returned, he told me that this was all for me. I said, "You're kidding, right?" He said, "They know all about you, Sheriff Green." My friend said that most of them have never seen a sheriff of law enforcement or even heard of a sheriff, period, but, "You are big, a big man to them." I was so humbled that I became speechless and emotional to the point that I could not hold back the tears. This was the second time I had been treated with such great honor. The other time was during my visit to South Africa.

As we continued to meet officials from the government of South Korea, we were driven to our hotel in a Mercedes Benz. After we got settled in our hotel, my friend and I went to a dinner arranged by my friend's brother who is a senator (I was not prepared for that). As we arrived for dinner at Seoul's number one dinner restaurant, the crowd of dignitaries stood, clapping their hands to welcome me to dinner, and yes, I was wearing my sheriff's uniform as my hosts had requested. I felt as if I were the President of the United States, meeting top congressional officials at the White House, but I was in South Korea. What a wonderful feeling of acceptance! I was

greeted with handshakes, hugs, and pats on the back. I felt so humble, weak, and speechless. I could not believe this dinner and greeting were for me. I took lots of photos and signed autographs as I kept trying to convince myself all this was not for me. After all, I'm not an important dignitary; I'm just a regular law enforcement officer, a sheriff from Kansas. That did not matter to the citizens of South Korea; for them, I was an important man.

After dinner, my friend took me on a tour to see one of the largest churches in the world, if not the largest. The Yoido Full Gospel Church of Seoul, Korea, had a membership of about 300,000 members when I visited in 2005. You may be wondering how all those members get to church on Sunday. Some drove their vehicles, some rode the public transit, and others walked to church, but most were picked up by public-transit-sized buses owned by the church. The parking lot looked like our public transit station in Kansas City, Missouri, with many buses—hundreds of buses one after another—unloading church members for service. To accommodate so many attendees, five church services were held on Sunday; as soon as one service was over, the next service would begin. To keep members nearby while they waited for the next service, the church has a coffee house, a small shopping center, book store, and other entertainment. In total, the Yoido Full Gospel Church complex consists of 12 components: (1) cross tower, (2) main sanctuary, (3) education building #1 with bookstore, (4) education building #2, (5) administration and world mission center, (6) another building, (7) Yoido Park, (8) Twin Towers and Yeouinaru Subway Station, (9) The 63 Building, (10) Lexington Hotel, (11) Yoido Hotel, and (12) the Han River.

We walked up the steps to enter the church so we could meet the pastor. As soon as I stepped onto the sanctuary floor, I was hit with what seemed like a bolt of thunder that knocked me to my knees; my legs, my arms, and my whole body lost all strength. I was so weak that I just fell to my knees in humble prayer. I realized that I was in the presence of God, so I started praying as tears ran down my cheeks; I was crying and praying for God to forgive me, for I have sinned. I kept praying, and when my friend saw what was happening, he fell to his knees and started praying as well. I have not had an experience like that in all my Christian life. God was truly in this house.

Then, it was time to meet the pastor of the Yoido Full Gospel Church of South Korea. It was a joy, physically and spiritually, to meet the pastor. He looked at me, smiled, and gave me a big hug, putting his hand on top of my head. Then, he started praying over me, saying, "God has work for you to do. Just keep trusting in God, for God will be calling you. You are my good friend." The pastor went on to say, "I have a gift for you." And the pastor prayed again for me and gave me a special gift, a Bible printed in Korean and English. (I still have that Bible.) As we said goodbye to each other, the pastor told me to keep this Bible with me. This was an experience I will never forget, a blessing from afar set up by God. Our next stop was one of the largest cities in South Korea, the city of Gimcheon, which is called the "City of Dreams."

We had one last stop to make after that. My friend wanted me to meet his sister at her church, and I agreed that would be fine. As we arrived at her church, I was stunned and surprised. I said, "Oh, my God"! I suddenly remembered that his sister's "church" is a Buddhist temple. My friend's sister is a Buddhist priest, and I'm thinking, "Oh no"! As we started walking up the steps to the front door, the Holy Spirit told me to look up, and as I looked up, I saw three animal heads that looked like wild beasts (statues of pagan gods). Each statue was looking down at us with its mouth open in a growling roaring position, as if it were ready to attack anyone entering the temple. This was a very frightening experience for me. As we continued closer to the church entrance, I was stopped in my tracks by what felt like a hard stiff-arm strike to my chest; I tried to move forward again and again with the same results, a hard thump in my chest stopping me in my tracks. I realized it was the Holy Spirit warning me not to go inside this temple, because the evil of Satan was lurking inside, waiting for those who enter. I looked over at my friend and said, "I can't go inside this temple." He asked, "Why?" I explained what just happened and said again, "I can't go in there." By that time, my friend's sister arrived and invited us to come inside her temple. I did not want to be rude, so I just said, "Hello. It's good to meet you. Sorry, but I can't go inside; I must leave. It was a pleasure to meet you." Then, I quickly made my exit back down the stairs. Once again, I told my friend, "I can't go inside because the Holy Spirit advised me to leave this place at once." So, he stopped in his tracks and said, "If you are not going in, I'm not going in either." We both turned to his sister and said our goodbyes and headed down the steps away from the Buddhist temple.

As we distanced ourselves from the temple, my spirit felt relief and was refreshed. I felt happy once again, and my mind was focused on helping people make the right decision in following Christ and doing what God wants us to do. That's when the Holy Spirit spoke to me, "You are now a minister of the Gospel. Go preach, teach, and witness to my word." To this day, that is what I have been doing. My script has been written by the Holy Spirit; I have a clear picture of what God has assigned me to do. I am to teach when the opportunity is available, to preach the word when confronted or asked, and of course to witness whenever possible in the name of our Lord and Savior Jesus Christ. I thank God for giving me the knowledge and the time and the patience as I witness to people with the right information to follow Christ according to the Word of God.

Thank God for the Holy Spirit who watches over us day and night. Thank you, Lord! Right now, I feel like shouting, shouting, and shouting, I feel like singing songs of praises to my Lord, and my God, my Savior. Where would I be if not for you, Lord? I have joy, joy, joy in my soul. Hmm, down at the cross where my savior died, down where for cleansing from sin I cried, there to my heart was the blood applied, singing glory to His name! I am so wondrously saved from sin. Jesus so sweetly abides within. There at the cross where he took me in; I'm singing glory to his name! I'm singing glory to his name! I'm singing glory to his name! Amen.

Chapter 7: Spiritual Therapy

One night as I slept, the Holy Spirit spoke to me through a dream, but I was unaware that the Holy Spirit was trying to contact me to deliver a message. When I awoke the next morning, I started the day off as usual. I was in the process of adding more material to this book from other events that occurred in my life. In the midst of this task, a strange feeling came over me, and everything within my immediate area just stopped—shut down to a complete silence, while the outside world went on functioning as usual. Strange as it may seem as I tell you this, I could not hear a sound from the outside. As thoughts were going through my mind, my thinking all went blank; my typing, my writing, and all functions just came to a sudden stop. I was not feeling very well at this point—I was not comfortable and not at peace with myself. As I struggled to figure out what had just happened, I felt like I was missing a piece of the puzzle. All of a sudden, a cold chilling feeling came over me as quietness entered the room. I immediately called on God for help. And God immediately answered my call, as a voice from heaven spoke to me in the quietness. It was the Holy Spirit sent by God to assist me in my troubles, sent to be my spiritual therapist to make me whole again.

I felt as though I was asleep, dreaming in a different time zone like the *Twilight Zone*. I listened very patiently as the Holy Spirit spoke to me saying, "You are about to enter into an area of your life called forgiveness. I was sent to stop you from continuing any further involving forgiveness. You are being stopped because you yourself have violated the rules of forgiveness. You have not forgiven those who have persecuted you during your life up to this present day." I awoke with a very heavy heart, and I felt sad and disturbed about my behavior pertaining to forgiveness. Looking back on my behavior toward people who had persecuted me in the past, I realized the Holy Spirit was right. I had not forgiven them. The Holy Spirit said that I must forgive all the people who had caused me harm, those who had damaged me physically and mentally with slanderous and false statements. I immediately fell to my knees in prayer, remembering what Jesus said at His crucifixion, "Father, forgive them, for they do not know what they do" (Luke 23:34). Then, I went into a deeper prayer saying, "Oh God, My God forgive me for I have sinned using hatred, meanness, bitterness, and anger as a tool to pay back those who have persecuted me, I am truly sorry, Oh Lord." At that moment, the spirit of forgiveness fell upon me like a thunderbolt from heaven. I humbled myself once again, forgiving all those I remember and all those I may have forgotten who have persecuted me from childhood to adulthood. I asked God to forgive them all as I prayed:

My Father in Heaven, I want to thank you for making this day and this moment possible, allowing me to go back into my life and clean up my act, to clean up my body, to clean up my mind and my soul, allowing me to bring back my focus to you Oh Lord and not on myself or my persecutors. Thank you, Lord. Thank you, God for making this day possible. In your son Jesus's name, Amen.

After my confession, the Holy Spirit spoke to me once again saying, "Now go finish your book; all is forgiven." Everything went back to normal as I continued writing, starting with this scripture:

Make a joyful shout to the LORD, all you lands! Serve the LORD with gladness; come before His presence with singing. Know that the LORD He is God; it is He who has made us, and not we ourselves; we are His people and the sheep of His pasture. Enter into His gates with thanksgiving; and into His courts with praise, be thankful to Him and bless His name. For the LORD is good; His mercy is everlasting, and His truth endures to all generations.

—Ps. 100:1–5

The Holy Spirit continued to guide me saying, "It's time for your therapy treatment." The Holy Spirit directed me to go to my files and pull out all those songs that I had written over the years. I was told to read each title and the lyrics of each song and then to meditate in prayer afterward. I did just that. As I read the song titles and lyrics, I felt like I was getting a full body massage spiritually because messages were being sent to me from the titles and lyrics. I felt as though I was getting a special treatment massage; I was truly feeling the healing sensation all through my body. Thank you, sweet Jesus. Suddenly, I felt the presence of the Holy Spirit relieving my body of stress, pain, and discomfort. I felt so weak from a therapeutic point of view that my body started breaking down and losing strength; my vision was getting weak, and my thinking was losing its sharpness. Suddenly, I felt the Holy Spirit starting to replace the elements that I was losing. He was replacing them with a relaxing atmosphere of peace, rest, and comfort along with joy and happiness; He was restoring my strength and my thinking to normal. My body and my mind were all back to normal as well.

I believe we all need a spiritual therapy session consistently, day-to-day, to bring us back down to earth, reminding us that we ourselves are still human and are still subject to the same daily struggles as everyone else. Thank God we have a spiritual doctor, the Holy Spirit, we can call on 24 hours a day for spiritual help and spiritual guidance to make us whole again. Amen and Amen. As I continued with my therapy, the Holy Spirit directed me to read the songs and messages that I had written. After that task was completed, the Holy Spirit said, "Go and meditate on each message and scripture at the top of each message." The songs and messages are listed nearby.

My Songs

1. The Power of the Spirit
2. Lord, I Need Thee
3. Forgive Me, Lord
4. God Can Fix It
5. For Me
6. No One Else
7. God Is Everywhere
8. I Understand
9. Be Alright
10. So Grateful
11. I Made It
12. Over There
13. I'm a Soldier
14. Running for Jesus

15. I Have Something to Say
16. I've Got Joy
17. A Song in My Heart
18. I'm Going Home
19. I Can't Wait
20. Praise Him, Amen
21. Can't Stay Here
22. Going to the Mountain
23. The Answer
24. Take Me Away
25. He's Calling Me
26. Sing and Shout All Day Long
27. Amen, Amen (praise hymn)
28. The Promise Land
29. Tell Somebody
30. One Day
31. He's Coming Back
32. Holy Ghost Fire
33. My Father's Train
34. Rise
35. The Cross Is Coming
36. He Got Up
37. My Jesus
38. Praising My Lord
39. When the Believers Come Home
40. The Lord's Table
41. When God Whispers
42. Save It for Me
43. My Destiny
44. In the Shadows
45. As I Walk into This World
46. I'm Not Tired Yet
47. God Is Saying
48. Get Out
49. Holy Ghost Spirit
50. Make Me Whole
51. Yes, Lord
52. Let's Do It
53. Another Day
54. Praise My God
55. Yes, He Is

My Messages

1. Subtitles—don't lose your shout:
   a. What am I shouting for?
   b. Where is my shout?
   c. Who let my shout out?
2. Stay on the wall
3. The key
4. Derailed
5. Changing faces; is it necessary?
6. Faith
7. When the fire falls/testimonies
8. In the wilderness it's time to come home
9. Knocking on the door "Who is it?"
10. To catch a thief
11. I am somebody
12. Main event
13. Give up the ghost
14. The recruit
15. Temptation/fear versus trust
16. The shepherd

17. The gladiator
18. Prison break
19. Freedom after a while
20. Are you ready to take the witness stand?
21. The battle is not over
22. Forgiveness is guaranteed by God
23. What's under your rock?
24. Obedience is the answer to Satan's bondage

I followed those orders from the Holy Spirit and, as I read and meditated, I felt a sense of spiritual strength and relief; I felt peace and comfort being restored in my body. The result was an energizing feeling that came over my body, putting me in a relaxed atmosphere of spiritual relief that brought happiness and joy. I could not have asked for a better physician or therapist than the Holy Spirit to take care of me. I thank God for sending the Holy Spirit. God knew from the start what I needed, a good old-fashioned spiritual flushing out of all the negative feelings that were boxed up inside me. I had an angry, payback-type attitude boiling inside of me all this time, which would have eventually caused health problems or death. When you listen to God and follow His directions, your rewards will be endless and priceless. I'm talking about being spiritually reborn—a new you, a new person, and a new spirit in Christ along with the gifts of the spirit such as peace, comfort, joy, happiness, kindness, and songs of praises that only God can bring. Here we go:

Hmm, Hmm, that's called spiritual therapy. Hmm, Hmm, right now I feel like preaching and praising God. Hmm, I feel like shouting. Hmm, I feel like clapping my hands. Hmm, I feel like stomping my feet. Hmm, I feel like dancing and singing praising to the Almighty God. Hmm, do you know him? Hmm, do you know him? Hmm, say yes . . . Hmm, say yes . . . Hmm, say yes. Hmm, don't you fool me. Hmm, do you know him? Hmm, he's a father when you need a shoulder to lean on. Hmm, he's a mother when you are sick and not feeling well. Hmm, he's a brother and a sister. Hmm, a friend in times of trouble. Hmm, a doctor when you have health problems. Hmm, a lawyer when things go wrong and folks try to take advantage of you. Hmm, God is right there by your side standing shoulder to shoulder. Hmm, he's right there. Hmm, he's right there. Hmm he's right there. I know he is; yes, he is. He's right there by your side—the Almighty God, the all-powerful God, the God of heaven and earth, my God, your God, and our God the Almighty God. Amen, Amen, and Amen.

Chapter 8: My Ordination

I received my calling to the ministry in 2003 during my membership at Evangelistic Center. Initially, I did not recognize my calling or understand the vision that I was receiving spiritually through dreams. At that point of my life, I had no knowledge or training in recognizing gifts of the Holy Spirit or the spiritual dreams that I received. I just did not pay that much attention to the Holy Spirit at that time in my walk with God. The lack of knowledge and experience about how the Holy Spirit works and speaks to us through dreams and visions cost me dearly in the early stages of my spiritual walk with God. But as I continued to study and read my Bible, attend Sunday school, and progress through ministry training, I became more knowledgeable of the Word of God. I became more interested in how the Holy Spirit works and speaks to us through our dreams and visions. During my ministry training program, I was overwhelmed by a passion to learn more about the Word of God and to use that training to help others find God.

During my training and ordination process, I became more concerned and more passionate to teach and tell others about the Word of God. I decided that there was something I had to do before I could continue with my training. I had to allow God to come into my life and wash me clean of all my sins because I was dirty and needed a spiritual bath, a spiritual makeover to make me whole. I experienced a change in my life after my spiritual bath; tears flowed down my cheeks on a regular basis. I was at peace, and my emotions were intense, especially when I heard certain gospel songs and when our pastor preached on certain topics about Christ and our lives as Christians. I became more responsible for my actions, recognizing the difference between good and evil, love and hate, friend and enemy, rich and poor, sick and the healthy, husband and wife, and worldly treasures and Godly treasures. I was more attuned to the Father, the Son, and the Holy Spirit.

After I graduated from my ordination program, I became a Sunday school teacher. I taught a class titled "How to Maintain Our Bodies through Spirit and Exercise." Teaching Sunday school gave me a wonderful opportunity to learn more about the Word of God than I had learned from my Catholic upbringing and other ministries. I was learning while I taught my class. As an ordained minister, I know that we have the freedom to choose our beginning and ending by following God, not the world. I have something more to offer than just coming to church on Sundays, singing in the choir, and going to Sunday school. I did not know the magnitude of my calling at first, but as I received more training and taught Sunday school, God allowed me to become more knowledgeable about His Word. By teaching and ministering the gospel of our Lord and Savior, Jesus Christ, I became a better servant of God.

Then, I learned to recognize my gifts as the Spirit touched me with spiritual songs of praise and a spiritual message for each song. In the beginning of this journey, I got very confused: I got preaching, teaching, and witnessing for our Lord and Savior mixed up. That is, I thought my calling was to be a preacher standing behind the podium delivering messages to a congregation, and I believed that for quite some time. My reasoning came from individuals in the community, especially friends and relatives, who typically addressed me as a preacher: "Hey, reverend," "Hey, preacher," or "Hey, bishop." I know now, thank God, that their greetings were no calling from God. As the Holy Spirit continued to give me messages about the direction I should go, I understood that my calling was not to be a preacher/pastor of a church, but to be a witness, a missionary, and a teacher of God's Word across this land. I believe it was God's plan for me to get training and credentials before hitting the road for Him. And, of course, the spiritual message I received from the Holy Spirit was realized as Christ gave me the opportunity to share the gospel in other countries such as South Africa and South Korea and in California, New York, and Texas. What a wonderful spiritual feeling I gained from experiencing the gifts of the spirit of joy, peace, and love. These are the gifts of God that we Christians use as we walk with God witnessing to the unsaved.

Many of the people to whom I witnessed have not yet accepted Christ in their lives, and some have no idea of the magnitude of what it is like to be a child of God. But now that they have heard the word, they have an opportunity to accept Christ and experience the joy, love, and kindness that other Christians feel. I offer this prayer to God:

Thank you, God for this day and this opportunity and thank you for your son Jesus, who died on the cross on Calvary's mountain for us. Oh Lord, here we go: Hmm, but on that third day morning, on that third day morning, our Lord got up. He got up; yes, he did. He got up yea, yea, yea with all power in his hands—all power, all power, in his hands. Yes, he did; yes, he did. I'm so happy; I'm so happy that he did not leave me alone. Amen, Amen, and Amen.

I had no idea that being a witness and a child of God was a full-time job, 7 days a week. On Sunday, we bring in our vehicles, our bodies, to church service, which is our spiritual fueling station. In corporate worship, God, with the help of the Holy Spirit who is His special mechanic, fills us up again with the Spirit of God, beating out all the dents, bumps, and scratches our bodies have absorbed during our walk with God. We may come into church with the equivalent of spiritual fender benders barely able to move forward, engine failures that keep us from getting started, low or flat tires reflected in our weary bodies, steering problems that prevent us from staying on the straight and narrow road, and lost in an unfriendly world without a spiritual road map. Oh, but God, but God who has the best mechanic in this world will get us home where we can lay our worn-out bodies down and get some rest. Early on Sunday morning, God will wake us up for our service call. As we enter the front doors of the church, the Holy Spirit descends on us with hymns of praise and worship and prayer time as we pray to God for healing while our choir of angels sing songs of praises, refreshing our bodies and spirits. Look out; here we go again:

Oh, God of heaven, Oh God of this world, our everlasting Father. Peace be unto you, Oh Lord, and peace be upon this earth. Let the church say Amen. Let the church say, "Amen." God has spoken. Let the church say, "Amen."

When the pastor gives the message, our battery (our spirit) is fully charged for another week of travel, and we say, "Thank you, Lord; Thank you, Lord." From all my training, I learned how to separate love from hate, good from evil, the truth from a lie, trust from false statements, and friend from enemy. Always remember that God will be right there; He will never leave you alone. God is our Father; we are His sons and daughters.

I have a better understanding of God's plans for me. My travels around the world were God's way of preparing me for the dangers ahead during my tour of duty in law enforcement, ministry, and social gatherings where temptation awaited me daily. Remember that Satan will tempt us around the clock with greed and sexual favors; Satan never stops. If not for the Lord on my side, where would I be? I will continue to praise and worship the Lord, day in and day out, because Jesus is my rock, Jesus is my sword, Jesus is my shield, Jesus is my wheel in the middle of a wheel. He guides my footsteps, and when I feel down and sad, Jesus wipes away all my tears and restores my smile and my joy. Do you know Jesus? Do you know Jesus? Yes, I do know Jesus. Amen and Amen.

Chapter 9: Sheriff and Ordained Minister of God

For about 15 years, I was both a sheriff and an ordained minister of God, and I struggled to decide which of these roles would be the authority in my life. In this chapter, I explore this battle for authority in my life. Before I could decide, I had to consider the factors involved in both roles: power, authority, trust, honesty, kindness, fairness, obedience, decision-making, greed, and temptation. I asked myself, "Which of the two titles requires these characteristics?" Of course, both positions require roughly the same characteristics and qualifications if one is to be a trustworthy leader who can be held to a higher standard every day.

I worked hard to balance the demands of being both a law enforcement official and an ordained minister. I felt that I needed to choose one or the other, but the decision was not an easy one. Satan was constantly knocking on my door trying to get me to choose the position with more glamour, more excitement, more money, and more gifts under the table. I resisted these temptations every day, trying to avoid favoritism from high officials, friends, relatives, and from others who were seeking favors. My conscience would not let me do what Satan wanted. Sometimes, he came at me in disguise, such as a basketful of gifts, a checkbook with lots of money, and an offer saying, "You don't even have to come to work every day, you will still get your salary." That was a lot of temptation to deal with day after day. The only answer was prayer, prayer, and more prayer, asking God to help me make the right decisions that would benefit everyone.

Honesty and fairness were a big part of my life and career. Even when times were rocky, I decided to stay faithful to God and do things God's way.

I never forgot what God had done for me when my ship was sinking and all seemed lost; He pulled me off that sinking ship onto fertile, dry land. Thank you, Lord. As a result, I understand that God is always in control; no matter what our circumstances may be, God is always in control. Our titles mean nothing to God; they are just titles. My titles will never outweigh my faith in God. Certainly, I had opportunities to switch sides and go for the world's glory, giving orders, taking gifts, and accepting favors just to get support and look good in public. But I reminded myself that worldly treasures meant nothing because I know that God is greater than any worldly treasures that man has to offer. I know that God is always in control. In the struggle between my job titles—sheriff or minister, which one wins? My answer: It's a tie. Neither wins; both titles are working for God in the person of LeRoy Green Jr. Whether sheriff or minister, the titleholder is a Christian working in God's army, helping people turn their lives around and accept Jesus Christ as their Lord and Savior. God gets all the glory, and we get blessings from God. So, if you are having problems with your identity, trust in God, and He will help you make the right choice for your life. No one else can do what God can do, no one else.

Chapter 10: Living with Spiritual Joy

It has been a joy for me to write this book about my life to let the world know that although we may start life's journey on the wrong foot, living a worldly life, we have no idea what the ending will be. We may face challenges in life—struggles, pain and suffering, wrongful pleasures, hardships, and lots of disagreements. Over time, we learn that living a worldly life is not as easy as one might expect. When all was said and done, I was frozen in my tracks like a deer caught in the headlights of an oncoming vehicle. Before I found Christ, I was caught in the headlights of this world, which seemed full of excitement, entertainment, party fun, sexual promiscuity, drugs, and alcohol.

With the world's attractions at my disposal, going along with the flow was the easiest thing to do. To be honest, I did not know what to do at first. By joining in the worldly lifestyle, I put a sign on my back, saying, "Open season, I'm a new guy in this worldly game." I was attacked from all angles by all the beasts of this worldly jungle. Why? Because I was a freshman in worldly lifestyle, not knowing the different weapons that the world uses to keep the lifestyle going. I had no weapons to defend myself from attacks by this worldly beast. Gradually, I learned that going into this wilderness of parties, drinking, sexual activities, dancing, and clubbing unprepared is like committing suicide at a slow pace. Such worldly activity leads to tremendous damage to a person's mind, body, and soul. I found that danger was always lurking just outside the party door. After seeing numerous deadly confrontations in nightclubs and house parties, I was fully aware of the dangers.

Freedom in Christ

Thankfully, when everything else had failed and I had nowhere else to go, I realized that my party days were likely to come to an end in a horrifying way, where death would be the only outcome. I had no choice but to fall on my knees with humility and shame, making a decision to call on God. That is why I say that by trusting and putting your faith in the Almighty God—whatever your trouble or circumstance or past history—God will still be there right by your side when it's all over. God will take care of all your faults, your troubles, your pain and suffering, your ups and downs. With assurance, I can say, "Thank you, Lord for all you have done for me. My dreams and wishes have come true, and I am so happy that I decided to turn my life over to you Lord."

Now, I can help people who are going through the same or similar problems as I experienced. I can witness to them and tell them what God has done for me, hoping my testimony will help them turn their lives around so they can also witness for God. Accepting Christ changes everything: people begin to live better lives and turn away from the dangerous activities of the party life. I will forever give God all the praise and all the glory. I have no greater love but to love my Lord and Savior Jesus Christ, the Lord is my Shepherd, and I am His sheep.

As I write this, it's Easter, and I am reminded of what Christ suffered for you and me as I watch the movie, *The Passion of Christ*. The movie reminds us that Christ suffered when the soldiers beat Him badly with whips that had nails and wire attached so the barbs would stick into Jesus's flesh ripping it from His body. And at the same time, soldiers continually beat and punched Jesus's face as blood flowed from a crown of thorns pressed into His scalp. Nevertheless, Jesus carried the cross, even though He sometimes stumbled and fell under its weight. Jesus never gave up. Jesus gave His life for you and me to cover our sins. Despite the cruelty He endured, Jesus still had forgiveness in His heart as He prayed, "Father, forgive them for they know not what they do." Then, Jesus died. Jesus's tormentors thought He was dead forever and that they had won. But on the third day, the greatest miracle occurred:

> *Hmm, but on that third day morning, . . . Jesus got up. He got up. Yes, he did with all power in his hands—all power in his hands. He got up with all power in his hands. Amen.*

Had I not forgiven my tormentors during my career, I don't believe the Holy Spirit would have directed me to write this book. God waited for me to show forgiveness to my tormentors before He could use me. Colossians 3:12–13 describes the character of the new man:

> **Therefore, as the elect of God, holy and beloved, put on tender mercies, kindness, humility, meekness, longsuffering; bearing with one another, and forgiving one another, if anyone has a complaint against another; even as Christ forgave you, so you also must do.**

When I complied with God's Word, forgiving my tormentors, the Holy Spirit said to me, "Now, go tell your story." I felt so relieved with joy in my heart that I labeled that day as my third-day morning—the day when I got up . . . I got up . . . oh yes, I got up, to finish the job that God had appointed me to do. I have the power of joy in my soul, I have the power joy in my hands, I have the power of joy in my feet, and I have power of joy in my speech. Even when I was in captivity in the system, I still had joy. Joy is a very important factor not only in my life, but in your life as well. Even in my day-to-day life, I considered myself in captivity to a certain degree. Although I was not bound in shackles and chains or placed behind bars in a dungeon, I faced other forms of captivity and issues that kept me hostage throughout my life and career. These captivities were not visible to the naked eye. Rather, these forms of captivity came from Satan with his legion of evil spirits who came after me daily, disguised as "Mr. and Mrs. Friendly." Today, I am free; I can shout with joy about finding and calling my God, my Lord and my Savior for help. God came to my rescue with His army of angels, and He destroyed "Mr. and Mrs. Friendly" and all my problems, bringing joy back into my life. That is why I say that joy is a very important factor in my life, yes even in captivity.

I have learned that when I wake up in the morning with the joy of God in my heart, my everyday problems and struggles are nothing. As a result, I always find time to praise God for what He has already done and what He is getting ready to do. I experience joy every time I talk to God; I can't help but smile. Even before I speak a word, I'm already smiling; God makes me feel happy! Don't ever try to fight the opposition by yourself because you will lose the battle every time. When you turn all your troubles and problems over to God, you will have peace and joy, and you will win every time.

My Special Gift—My Wife

Indeed, it is a joy to find and taste what paradise is all about when you put your faith in God and trust Him. On November 14, 2009, I was wonderfully blessed when God gave me a special gift, someone to stand by my side. My special gift is my angel, my wife Lonia Green, the very lovely, caring, passionate, and helpful lady God chose for me—to be my wife, my helpmate, my friend, and at times my advisor. She's always there ready to assist me in my ups and downs, my needs, and my decision-making. My wife is a beautiful woman inside and outside; I could not have asked for a better choice—God sure can pick them. When I wake up in the morning, the first thing I do is thank God for another day and then, I look at my wife who is usually still asleep and resting peacefully. I pause for a moment looking at her and then I whisper softly to myself:

> *Great day in the morning! This is all mine. Thank you, Lord for this beautiful gift, this beautiful woman you have given me. I could not have asked for or picked a better gift. Thank you, Lord. I will love, protect, serve, and cherish this gift, my wife, until death do us part. She's my angel, my joy, my helpmate. As I close, I want to say, thank you, Lord so much for lifting me out of the pits of hell, the kingdom of Satan.*

Spiritually Free and Whole

I no longer have to endure the pain, suffering, and trials of hardships in this mean old world because now, I have the Lord on my side. I still remember when I was held captive by this sinful world; I was on a path of destruction. I believe God saw something in me worth saving, and He sent His therapist, the Holy Spirit, to help me. In those days, I was not feeling whole; something was missing in my life. I was not comfortable or at peace within myself. But I prayed, asking God to help me. He answered my prayer by sending the Holy Spirit to help me become whole again. As

the Holy Spirit ministered to me, He directed me to go back to all the songs that I had written and read the titles and the lyrics of each song, and then pray and meditate. It worked. As I read the titles and lyrics of each song, a message of healing came back to me, massaging my spirit, relaxing my body in peace, rest, and comfort. And I shed tears of joy, cleansing my body as the Holy Spirit ministered to me. The Holy Spirit took away all the stress, pain, and suffering. I felt whole again, I felt joy, I felt happiness, and I felt peace within my soul.

Finally, I want to thank all those pastors with whom I had the opportunity and privilege to serve. They taught me the basics of what it means to be a Christian, a worker for God, a friend in times of need, and a shepherd when a word from God is needed. I thank all those pastors for teaching me to be direct and forceful, using the gifts that God has given me. I thank my pastor, Dr. Ricky D. Turner, for modeling honesty, patience, and trust in God.

If the Lord had not been on my side when all other options failed, I would have been lost because there was nothing anyone else could do. But God was right there by my side from day one; God came and rescued me and lifted me out of the pits of hell. God cleaned me up and gave me a new wardrobe and lots of songs of praise. Oh, I feel like preaching right now. Where would I be, where would I be, had it not been for the Lord on my side? All I can say right now while I'm singing is:

Father, Father, Father, Father, Father, Father, Father, Father, Father, Father is his name—Jesus, Jesus, Jesus, Jesus, Jesus, Jesus, Jesus, Jesus, Jesus, Jesus is His name—Holy Ghost, Holy Ghost, Holy Ghost, Holy Ghost, Holy Ghost, Holy Ghost, Holy Ghost, Holy Ghost, Holy Ghost, Holy Ghost is His name. I'm so happy now because I did not give up. I did not give up. I held onto the Father's hand; I held onto the Father's hand. Through the storms and through the rains, the thunder and lightning, through the heartaches and pain, through the day-to-day suffering, I still held onto the Father's hand. Oh Lord, Oh my God, when I have sung, when I have sung my last song, and I have prayed my last prayer, it's time for me to go home and be with my Lord because I have been redeemed, bought with a price, with the help of the Holy Spirit, I've turned my whole life around praising God.

As I close, I want to say a special message to my children: I love you all very much.

This is my story. May God be the glory. Amen, Amen, and Amen.

Milestones in the Life
of LeRoy Green Jr.

1968   139-pound Golden Gloves Novice Champion

1969   Graduate of Bishop Ward High School

1972   147-pound Golden Gloves Open Champion

1978   160-pound Midwest Middleweight Professional Boxing
       Champion Rank #17

1978   Sworn in as a Wyandotte County Deputy Sheriff

1979   Graduate of Kansas Law Enforcement Academy,
       Hutchinson, Kansas

1982   Certified Defensive Tactics Instructor, Kansas Law
       Enforcement Academy

1985   Promoted to Sergeant

1985   Received Green Belt in Martial Arts Tae Kwon Do

1986   Graduate of Major Case Squad Investigation School
1995   Promoted to Undersheriff, Second in Command
1997   Graduate of 189th Session of the FBI National Academy
1999   Appointed Sheriff (first African American Sheriff in Kansas)
2001   Elected Sheriff of Wyandotte County, Kansas City, Kansas
2003   Ordained as a Minister of the Gospel
2005   Re-elected as Sheriff of Wyandotte County, Kansas City, Kansas
2006   Received Honorary 3rd Degree Dan Black Belt in Tae Kwon Do (South Korea)
2009   Married Lonia (the Most Beautiful Woman in the World)
2009   Retired from Sheriff's Department after 31 years

Deputy to receive award

Sgt. Leroy Green Jr. will receive a law enforcement award Sept. 21 from the Delaware Crossing Chapter, Sons of the American Revolution.

Sgt. Green of the Wyandotte County Sheriff's Department will receive the award at the chapter's breakfast meeting Sept. 21 at the Milburn Country Club, Overland Park.

Clarence Kelley, former director of the Federal Bureau of Investigation, will be the speaker at the meeting.

In nominating Sgt. Green for the award, Sheriff John L. Quinn cited his hard work in developing the tag registration program.

"He issues more tickets than anybody in our department, but he's always tactful about it," Sheriff Quinn said. "I've never had a complaint about him in the four years I've worked with him. People tell me, 'He gave me a ticket, but he was nice.' "

Sgt. Green, a 7-year veteran of the sheriff's office, is assigned to the city-county tag enforcement program.

Recent estimates from the county treasurer's office has indicated that this special program has resulted in nearly $600,000 in additional personal property money being collected.

Sgt. Green has worked as a coordinator for the program for the sheriff's department since its start three years ago.

In addition to his regular duties, Sgt. Green serves as a defensive tactics instructor for the department's training division.

He is a professional boxer and has completed 40 hours of testing to receive certification as a self-defense instructor in Kansas. He is currently working toward a black belt ranking in martial arts.

Sgt. Leroy
Green Jr.

* "Deputy to receive award," *The Wyandotte West*, September 19, 1985.

Green returns from FBI academy an inspired man

By ANDY WILLIAMS
of The Kansan

INSPIRED!!!

That's the best way to describe Wyandotte County Undersheriff Leroy Green who returned recently from the FBI academy in Quantico, Va.

"It was an opportunity I will always be thankful for and an experience that will have a positive effect on me for the rest of my life," Green said of his 11-week session at the nation's top law enforcement training facility.

Green was the first person from the sheriff's department to attend the academy, an honor he hopes will open the doors for others in the department.

"They told me there is an open door at the academy for our department. I'm going to encourage others from our staff to attend when it is possible. It truly is a wonderful experience."

Sheriff Mike Dailey, who attended the academy in 1995 while he was a Kansas City, Kan., police officer, said there was a notable change in Green since returning.

"It got him pumped up," Dailey said of the undersheriff. "Leroy has always been a go-getter but the experience has enhanced that. When he returned he hit the ground running and is in the process of instituting new training classes for our deputies."

While at the academy Green attended a variety of management, legal issues and public relations courses. He said his favorite class was called "Analytical Aspects of Criminal and Community Behavior."

"It taught us about profiling criminals based on their behavior. The course teaches you to look at the community differently," Green said. "It really caught my interest."

One of the more grueling aspects of the academy, the physical training, was not a problem for Green, a former professional boxer who remains fit.

"I was ready for it," Green said.

"They put you through the ropes but I was fine. The course work was the challenging part for me."

Green said it was tough to attend the courses and be successful after being away from school for 25 years. He said writing term papers was a skill he had to learn to master again.

"Believe it or not writing was the challenge. I had to work at it but I did OK. I typically got an A or a B on my papers but I worked at it," Green said.

Green said he was helped by courses Dailey sent him to prior to attending the academy. Green said he attended various courses at different colleges and seminars in the area. He said they helped him prepare for the challenge.

"They do not make it easy on you at the academy," Dailey said. "You have to be prepared and committed when you are accepted and finally go. Leroy's preparation and his desire to be successful helped him make it through."

(See GREEN, page 2A)

New sheriff settles in

By MIKE BELT
of the Kansan

The office is bigger. The telephone rings a little more frequently and the decisions he makes carry more weight, but otherwise Wyandotte County Sheriff Leroy Green hasn't felt much different than he did when he was the undersheriff.

"I haven't really had time to sit down and think about it," Green said Monday, a little more than a week after he was sworn in as sheriff.

"Maybe that's a good thing," he then added with a laugh.

Don't expect to see Green switch from wearing a uniform to a business suit now that he is the sheriff.

LEROY GREEN

Green has been wearing the sheriff's department blue uniform since he started his career 21 years ago and he says he will continue. Most sheriffs in recent history have worn suits.

"I think it sets an example to the others in the department that we should wear our uniforms and it lets the public know who we are," he said.

Green was sworn into office Sept. 2 after his predecessor, Mike Dailey, unexpectedly resigned to pursue outside interests.

Green picked Rick Mellott, another long-time deputy, to be his undersheriff. Mellott, previously a captain and supervisor in the jail's administrative support division, said Monday he hasn't had to make any major adjustments to his new position.

(See GREEN, page 2)

Green

(Continued from page 1)

"No, mainly because I've been a supervisor since 1976 and I've held every rank in the department," he said. "It's not a big change."

Mellott also noted that many of the senior ranking officers in the department have worked together and know each other, which makes his job easier.

When Green took over for Dailey he said he didn't expect to make a lot of changes. One area he does hope to improve is the jail booking process.

"We're looking at some options to speed up the booking process a little bit," he said. "That's one of our main objectives right now. That's something we need to address."

It takes an average of one to two hours to book someone into the jail, according to Green.

The sheriff also wants to start a mentoring program to help department employees who might be having problems. He said he wants deputies and employees to be able to talk about those problems. He hopes that will help cut down on turnover.

"We can't compete with the other agencies that pay more, but we can make it a point to listen to our employees and pay more attention to them," he said.

* Mike Belt, "New sheriff settles in," *The Kansan*.

Sheriff says court ruling opened doors

❏ *Sheriff discusses progress in meeting department's goals*

By ANDRE RILEY
Kansan staff writer

Fresh off two years of court and legislative battles with the Unified Government, Wyandotte County Sheriff Leroy Green Jr.

said his department is beginning to achieve the goals he set during his 1999 election campaign.

"We don't have to worry about court battles. It has opened the door to let us do our job," said Green. "When we do our job, we save the county money."

In an interview in his office at the Wyandotte County Justice Center, Green discussed the

state of the Sheriff's Department and its goals for the upcoming year.

"I've had this on my heart for a long time," Green said.

In June 2002, Green and the UG reached a settlement in U.S. District Court that allowed him to hire the juvenile and adult administrators, effectively giving the Sheriff's Department

(See GREEN, page 10)

JEREMY BANKS / Kansan photographer
SHERIFF LEROY GREEN

Green

(Continued from page 1)
control of the jail. The UG had contended the Jail Population Committee, which oversaw the jail, had the right to hire and fire administrators.

The settlement was followed by Legislative Auditor Tom Standish's report in July that Green could hire more than a 195-employee limit, set by the UG, and stay within his $13.5 million budget.

Changes in the department

Since then Green has set about many changes within the department including restructuring the command staffs of the department administration and the jail, enacting pay raises for officers above the rank of lieutenant and filling vacancies within the jail.

One of the first changes was the permanent hiring of Randall Henderson and Brad Ratliff as administrators of the adult and juvenile jail. The two had served on an interim basis, with pay rates below the position's listed salary, for nearly a year before the settlement.

The sergeant rank was also added to the department hierarchy between the deputy and lieutenant ranks. Before the change some deputies, the lowest rank in the Sheriff's Department, were being paid more than lieutenants.

Pay was subsequently raised for lieutenants to balance the inequity. Green feels the addition is key to improving training within the department.

"There was too much space between ranks. As sergeants, that is where you get your training as a supervisor," he said.

Overall, the rise of budgeted

positions, from 195 to 215, has allowed the department to begin staffing adequately.

For the first time in two years the Juvenile Detention Center has the filled the 48 positions required for the facility by law. While Green could not immediately divulge the total number of employees, he notes the number of deputies since the addition has increased to 128, which is 16 short of capacity.

In addition, the Sheriff's Department has begun forming a pool of applicants, making it easier to fill a vacancy if an employee leaves unexpectedly.

Budget savings

Despite all the changes, Green claims the department was nearly $1.1 million under budget in 2002.

The savings show the determination of the department to stay within budget to the UG, said Green.

"(The financial outlook) looks very promising," he said. "They can see from what we've done that we mean business."

The surplus has come using a variety of methods, according to Green. As an example, he says the department was able to renegotiate farm-out prices for inmates from $50 to under $30, a savings of $20 per inmate.

Farm-outs occur when an inmate is sent to another institution because of overcrowding or understaffing at their

home jail.

Money was also saved through procurement agreements. Bar soap for the jail facility is donated by Colgate Palmolive. The jail also buys equipment from the Federal Surplus store in Topeka.

Handling prisoners

Inmate management also underwent numerous changes in 2002. Among the most important, said Green, was the addition of inmate photos to security armbands and the Jail Management System. The updated armbands, required for every inmate, allow quick identification of an offender. Meanwhile, the management system will notify staff if an offender has warrants in other jurisdictions before they are released.

Improved accuracy in handling prisoners is the goal, said Green.

"We have to be careful not to let the wrong person go," he said. "If (a deputy) has any

> ❏ **"It takes seven years to get your program in place and we've got three more years for that. Even if I'm here by myself, we're going to do it."**
>
> *– Sheriff Leroy Green Jr.*

The year 2002 was very challenging for the motivated professionals of the Wyandotte County Sheriff's Department. We encountered many obstacles; some were internal, others were external; however, we demonstrated the dedication and ability to accomplish many goals. It is truly a privilege and a pleasure to be associated with motivated, dedicated, flexible, hardworking and assertive employees that represent the Wyandotte County Sheriff's Office. As a team, we have continually prevailed, even against strong opposition, setting a foundation for unlimited success. We will continue to be proactive while solving problems and analyzing fact that, in our quest to provide a quality service to our customers.

---

* Andre Riley, "Sheriff says court ruling opened doors," *The Kansan*.

One of the new security cameras installed at the jail is located in the holding area.

doubts, it's 'Let's see the armbands.'"

Ten-hour shifts were also instituted to provide around-the-clock coverage for inmates.

According to Sheriff's Department statistics, inmates with municipal charges worked more than 6,212 hours, or roughly 258 days, in the jail in 2002. Although the bulk of the work included painting and cleaning inside the jail, Green is exploring ways to take the program outside as well.

Green thinks community service work, which is similarly employed using Lansing Correction Facility inmates at the UG Fleet Center, could benefit all.

"It's worked very well," he said. "If there is anyway we can get folks out quicker through community service then we should do that. ... We need to get with the District Attorney and judges and see what they can do."

Suicide knives were also purchased by the department to free inmates who may attempt to take their lives. Although suicide has not been a problem, said Green, precautions are still necessary.

"If you don't have them and something happens, it's 'I told you so,'" Green said.

Goals for 2003

Green's goals for 2003 include continuing to boost staff morale by increasing interaction with management, keeping down operating costs and working to achieve certification of every department member.

Morale enhancing activities such as monthly potluck dinners and a revised, 12-step discipline program have led to a lower turnover rate, Green said.

Ratliff said it's all part of a philosophy to make the Sheriff's Department a career choice for Wyandotte Countians.

"We have normal turnover and lots of applicants," he said. "We trying to make this a choice of a career."

Certification for each employee is a priority because, Green said, it allows him to shift employees from one area to another based on need. In a war or other violent situation, Green wants to be ready.

"We're going to need folks that are well trained to help the city when this thing hits," he said.

Green hopes to create a family atmosphere in the Sheriff's Department.

"We've taken away all the negatives that people have. If they have any problems, I said let me know about it," Green said.

"Am I my brother's keeper, yes we are."

Ratliff said last year's battles to increase pay and staffing affected the entire department.

"Lots of times when things are slow to come it gets people impatient," he said. "Now the staff sees hope and they're having a easier time doing their jobs."

At a recent conference of sheriffs in Topeka, Green listened as one attendee stated that it normally takes seven years to effectively implement a management program.

When Green recounted the story to a visitor, a broad smile came across his face.

"It takes seven years to get your program in place and we've got three more years for that," he said. "Even if I'm here by myself, we're going to do it."

As for the future of his political career, possible a run at mayor, Green said that is out of his hands.

"I haven't had a chance to be sheriff yet. I haven't had a chance to finish this job first," said Green. "It has to be ordained from a spiritual standpoint. If the good Lord wants me to be mayor, then he'll make the opportunity available to me."

* Andre Riley, "Sheriff says court ruling opened doors," *The Kansan*.

Sheriff Leroy Green To Be Honored By African American Democratic Caucus

On Friday, Feb. 27, Sheriff Leroy Green Jr. will be honored by the African American Democratic Caucus of Kansas, the African American Democratic Caucus of Shawnee County and the Topeka branch of the NAACP as an African American Pioneer in Current Elected Office.

This honor will highlight the increasing members of the African American Community in new levels of achievement in communities across Kansas.

Sheriff Green has served the Wyandotte County community for over 30 years. Sheriff Green has been the Wyandotte County Sheriff since 1999 and is the first African American Sheriff elected in the state of Kansas. There will be a luncheon for the Sheriff and his family in his honor in Topeka, Kas.

LEROY GREEN JR.

Governor appoints Sheriff Green to task force

Sheriff Leroy Green Jr.

Task force members

■ Sheriff Leroy Green, Jr., was elected sheriff of Wyandotte County in 2001. He began working in the Wyandotte County Sheriff's Department in 1978, as a detention deputy in the jail. In 1982, he was given command of the Wyandotte County Tag Enforcement Unit. He served as a sergeant and undersheriff before being appointed sheriff in 1999. Sheriff Green was the first African-American sheriff in the State of Kansas.